POLICY AND PRACTICE IN EDUCATION

EDITORS

GORDON KIRK *AND* ROBERT GLAISTER

SPECIAL EDUCATIONAL NEEDS

Sheila Riddell

DUNEDIN ACADEMIC PRESS

EDINBURGH

Published by
Dunedin Academic Press Ltd
Hudson House
8 Albany Street
Edinburgh EH1 3QB
Scotland

ISBN 1 903765 12 9

British Library Cataloguing in Publication Data

A catalogue record for this book is available from the British Library

Typeset by Trinity Typing, Wark on Tweed
Printed in Great Britain by Cromwell Press

POLICY AND PRACTICE IN EDUCATION

NUMBER FIVE

SPECIAL EDUCATIONAL NEEDS

Margaret Sutherland.

© Carson-Dellosa

POLICY AND PRACTICE IN EDUCATION

CONTENTS

EDITORIAL INTRODUCTION

Education is now widely regarded as having a key contribution to make to national prosperity and to the well-being of the community. Arguably, of all forms of investment in the public good, it deserves the highest priority. Given the importance of education, it is natural that it should be the focus of widespread public interest and that the effectiveness and responsiveness of the educational service should be of vital concern to politicians, teachers and other professionals, parents and members of the general public. If anything, the establishment of Scotland's parliament, which has already affirmed education as a key priority, will witness an intensification of public interest in the nature and direction of educational policy and the changing practices in the schools. This series of books on *Policy and Practice in Education* seeks to support the public and professional discussion of education in Scotland.

In recent years there have been significant changes in every aspect of education in Scotland. The series seeks to counter the tendency for such changes to be under-documented and to take place without sufficient critical scrutiny. While it will focus on changes of policy and practice in Scotland, it will seek to relate developments to the wider international debate on education.

Each volume in the series will focus on a particular aspect of education, reflecting upon the past, analysing the present, and contemplating the future. The contributing authors are all well established and bring to their writing an intimate knowledge of their field, as well as the capacity to offer a readable and authoritative analysis of policies and practices.

The author of this volume, the fifth in the series, is Professor Sheila Riddell, who holds the Chair of Social Policy (Disability Studies) and directs the Strathclyde Centre for Disability Research at the University of Glasgow.

Professor Gordon Kirk
Faculty of Education
The University of Edinburgh

Dr Robert T D Glaister
School of Education
The Open University

ACKNOWLEDGEMENTS

This book refers to a number of research projects in which I have been involved over recent years. Chapters 2 and 3 draw on data from the ESRC funded project *The Justice Inherent in Special Educational Needs Assessments in England and Scotland*. My collaborators on this project were Professor Michael Adler and Dr Enid Mordaunt of the University of Edinburgh and Alastair Wilson of the Strathclyde Centre for Disability Research, University of Glasgow. Chapter 5 draws on data from the research project *Raising the Attainment of Pupils with Special Educational Needs* funded by the Scottish Executive Education Department. I collaborated on this project with Pauline Banks and Alastair Wilson of the Strathclyde Centre for Disability Research, University of Glasgow, Jean Kane of the St Andrew's Faculty of Education, University of Glasgow and Professor Alan Dyson, Dr Alan Millward and Anne Baynes of the Special Educational Needs Research Centre, University of Newcastle. I would like to thank all of these people for their contribution to the development of my thinking about disability and education. The interpretation of data in these chapters is my own.

Finally, I would like to thank Ken, Annie and Bella for their constant love and support.

CHAPTER 1

INTRODUCTION: THE HISTORICAL CONTEXT

Introduction: The purpose and focus of the book
Education for children with special educational needs (SEN) is an area of great importance not just for 'special education' professionals, but also for parents, children and young people and all those who have an interest in the broad field of education. Exploring the way in which mainstream education policies are experienced by those at the margins provides insights into the limitations or unintended consequences of these policies. Similarly, considering the type of provision made for disabled children and young people reveals a great deal about wider social values and priorities. The focus of the book is on the ways in which SEN policies and practices have developed from the eighteenth century to the present and the ways in which these are experienced at grass roots level by key players. Where appropriate, comparisons are made with policy and practice in England. Contrasting Scottish experience with that of other parts of the UK throws Scottish experience into relief and provides insight into the distinctiveness of the Scottish tradition.

The focus of the book is on SEN policy as it applies to children. There have also been important developments in policy and practice for young people in the post-16 age group. These are referred to, but the scope of the book does not allow for detailed discussion. The structure of the book is as follows. Chapter 1 provides a brief summary of the development of SEN policy and practice from the eighteenth century to the reports of the Warnock committee (DES, 1978) and of Scottish HMI (SED, 1978). This chapter explores the twin elements at play in provision for children with SEN. On the one hand, there has always been a desire to separate out children with SEN from others, emphasising distinctions between groups based on deficits. On the other hand, there has been a growing sense of social obligation to this group of pupils, accompanied by a recognition that, if they were to make progress, additional resources would have to be committed to their education. Similarly, from the earliest times tensions can be discerned between social inclusion and human capital imperatives. The latter suggests that the main purpose of education is to create social cohesion and develop shared norms and values, whilst the latter suggests that the rationale for state education is to contribute to the generation of wealth, with greatest investment being made in those who are likely to provide the best financial returns.

In Chapter 2, we consider the recent development of Scottish education policy for children and young people with SEN, making comparisons with English policy. Using a framework developed by Kirp (1982) it is argued that SEN policy in Scotland continues to be informed principally by the traditional frameworks of bureaucracy and professionalism, whereas English policy has been shaped by a wider range of policies including managerialism, marketisation, consumerism and legality. In Chapter 3, using four case study local authorities in Scotland and England, we discuss the way in which the different national frameworks were experienced in specific local contexts. It is evident that whilst national policies may look quite different in the abstract, when they are applied in real social settings they are transformed and subverted by the key players. Scottish policy is set up to minimise the role of the service consumer, whereas English policy, at least on paper, allows consumers a greater role. In practice, in both England and Scotland, socio-economic status has had a major influence on parents' level of involvement and, particularly for socially-disadvantaged families, appeared to over-ride attempts at consumer empowerment south of the Border.

In Chapter 4, the meaning of inclusion and links with the wider social inclusion policy framework are outlined. Different understandings of inclusion and debates between 'integrationists' and 'inclusionists' are explored. Data are presented on the placement of children with SEN in mainstream and special schools and units. Given the current emphasis on evidence-based policy, we consider what evidence would be needed to determine whether progress towards inclusion is taking place. Given the growth in the number of special units and the decline in the number of special schools, we suggest that it is very difficult to know whether inclusion policies are being successful, or are producing different forms of exclusion.

Chapter 5 focuses on the tension between social inclusion and raising attainment policies, both of which have formed a key part of New Labour's educational agenda. In line with social inclusion goals, it was decided to include children with SEN in the target-setting programme. The performance of most schools is measured in relation to children's performance in national tests and SQA examinations. However there has always been confusion about whether the performance of children with SEN should be included in the reporting of outcomes. Excluding children with SEN implies that their performance cannot be measured or is less relevant to assessing overall quality. Including them in overall judgements of a mainstream school's performance, however, may create perverse incentives, encouraging exclusion rather than inclusion. A solution promoted by the Scottish Executive was to assess the performance of children with SEN in terms of their attainment of long and short term targets specified within an Individualised Educational Programme (IEP). Children with SEN were also to be included within the wider target-setting programme. Drawing on evidence from a Scottish Executive funded project, this chapter considers the strengths and weaknesses of the target-setting initiative in relation to children with SEN and the implications for combining accountability and inclusion agendas.

Finally, Chapter 6 discusses the content and implications of the SEN and Disability Act 2001, which is now Part 4 of the DDA, coming into effect in September 2002. Since equal opportunities is a matter reserved to Westminster, this legislation covered Scotland, England and Wales, although it was implemented through separate national educational frameworks. The form which the legislation finally took, and the complexities of trying to apply common GB principles through different national legislative frameworks, are discussed. The wider implications of basing educational provision for children with SEN on rights rather than needs and the future implications of the legislation are considered.

Provision for children with SEN: early developments
The following paragraphs draw on reviews of historical developments undertaken by Tomlinson (1982) and the report of the Warnock Committee (DES, 1978). Educational provision for disabled children has been in existence for only a relatively short period of time. Establishments catering for children with sensory impairments were the first to emerge. In 1793, the Asylum for the Industrious Blind was founded in Edinburgh. Funded by social philanthropists, its aim was to provide vocational training for future employment, and it relied upon profits from workshops to cover its running costs. The first school for the deaf in Great Britain was opened by Thomas Braidwood in Edinburgh in the early 1760s. Mr Braidwood's Academy for the Deaf and Dumb (these two categories were regarded as indistinguishable) catered for a small number of fee-paying pupils. In 1783, the Academy moved to London where, in 1792, the first English school for the deaf opened with six children under the direction of Braidwood's nephew. Other Braidwood schools subsequently opened in major cities. Donaldson's Hospital (now school) for the Deaf in Edinburgh was opened in 1850.

Education for children with learning difficulties was slower to emerge. A school for the education of 'imbeciles' was established at Baldovan in Dundee in 1852; it later became Strathmartine Hospital. An institution for 'defectives' was established in Edinburgh, moving to a site in Larbert in 1863, where it was renamed the Royal National Scottish Hospital. The Luncay (Scotland) Act of 1862 recognised the needs of the 'mentally handicapped' and authorised the granting of licenses to charitable institutions established for the care and training of imbecile children.

Developments between1872 and 1945
The Education (Scotland) Act 1872 established school boards to provide elementary education in those areas where there were insufficient places in voluntary schools. The Act did not specifically include disabled children among those for whom provision was to be made. However, by 1874, 50 blind children were being educated in mainstream schools alongside their

peers. Disabled children who could be accommodated in mainstream schools would receive some education, but others who could not be accommodated would receive no schooling at all.

The lack of provision for such children caused increasing concern and in 1886 the Royal Commission on the Blind and Deaf was set up, chaired by Lord Egerton, an aristocrat with interests in the West Indian sugar business. The Commission report of 1889 concluded that: 'It is better for the state to expend its funds on the elementary technical education of the blind, than to have to support them through life in idleness'. The report underlined the economic arguments for educating disabled children and young people:

> The blind, deaf, dumb and the educable class of imbecile . . . if left uneducated, become not only a burden to themselves but a weighty burden on the state. It is in the interests of the state to educate them, so as to dry up, as far as possible, the minor streams which must ultimately swell to a great torrent of pauperism. (Egerton Commission, 1889)

In Scotland, legislation swiftly followed the report's publication. The Education of Blind and Deaf Mute Children (Scotland) Act of 1890 required authorities to make provision, in their own or other schools, for the education of blind and deaf children resident in their area who were not otherwise receiving suitable elementary education. Education for these children was to extend to the age of 16, much later than other children who might be given total or partial exemption form the age of eleven.

The Egerton Commission's Report distinguished between idiots, imbeciles and the feeble-minded. Whereas 'idiots' were regarded as ineducable and therefore should be retained in asylums or workhouses, it was believed that 'imbeciles', and 'the feeble-minded' could be taught basic tasks. In Scotland, the Education of Defective Children (Scotland) Act of 1906 empowered school boards to make provision in special schools or classes for the education of defective children between the ages of 5 and 16. It is interesting to reflect on the time lag between education for children with sensory impairments and those with cognitive difficulties. This is probably due to the fact that during the nineteenth century many children would be uneducated and illiterate. The gap between those with learning difficulties and others would therefore be much less marked.

The Mental Deficiency (Scotland) Act of 1913 required school boards to ascertain children in their area who were defective. Those who were considered incapable of benefiting from instruction in special schools were to be placed in an institution. This system of ascertainment quickly came to be regarded as stigmatising and many parents refused to present their children for assessment. In 1924, the Mental Deficiency Committee (the Wood Committee) recommended that there should be a closer association between special and mainstream schools and that special schools 'should be presented to parents not as something both distinct and humiliating, but as a helpful variation of the ordinary school'. By 1939, the number of mentally defective children on the roll of special schools and classes had reached 4,871.

The development of child guidance services and the Education (Scotland) Act 1945

During the first half of the twentieth century, there was a growing interest in psychometric testing to measure intelligence and to identify psychological problems. In Scotland in the late 1920s, an 'educational' clinic was opened by Dr William Boyd of the Education Department of the University of Glasgow and a 'psychological' clinic was established by Professor James Drever in the Psychology Department at Edinburgh University. The term 'child guidance clinic' was first used when the Notre Dame Clinic was opened in Glasgow. In 1937, Glasgow was the first education authority to establish a child guidance clinic on a full-time basis.

Developments between 1945 and 1978

The Education (Scotland) Act 1945 placed a general duty on education authorities to provide education for children which was suitable to their 'age, aptitude and ability'. In addition, there was a specific duty to establish which children, as a result of 'disability of mind or body', required 'special educational treatment' at school, including junior occupational centres, and which children were too handicapped to benefit from any form of education or training. To achieve this, parents could be required to submit their children for a medical examination (from 1969, extended to a psychological examination as well). Parents could appeal against a medical certificate which showed their child required special educational treatment and to the sheriff court against being refused permission to withdraw their child from special school. Education authorities were empowered (after 1969 required) to provide child guidance services and to provide 'special educational treatment'.

Regulations issued in 1954 defined the following nine legal categories of 'handicap' for which special educational provision should be made: deafness, partial deafness, blindness, partial sightedness, mental handicap, epilepsy, speech defects, maladjustment and physical handicap. The categories did not include children with milder learning difficulties, nor those whose difficulties stemmed from such factors as absenteeism or frequent change of school. The Schools (Scotland) Code 1956 laid down maximum class sizes for the various categories of handicap so as to ensure that pupils in special schools got more individual attention. There continued to be some ambivalence about how many children were to be given 'special educational treatment'. The Scottish Education Department in a 1955 circular indicated that it did not envisage a large scale system of separate special schools:

It is recognised that there must continue to be situations where it is essential in children's interests that the handicapped must be separated from those who are not. Nevertheless as medical knowledge increases and as general school conditions improve it should be possible for an increasing proportion of pupils who require special educational treatment to be educated along with their contemporaries in ordinary schools. Special educational treatment should be regarded simply as a well-defined arrangement within the ordinary educational system to provide for the handicapped child the individual attention that he particularly needs. (SED Circular 3000, 1955 (para 4).

Educational services were particularly slow to develop for 'maladjusted' children. The development of child guidance clinics focused more attention on their needs and from 1933, approved schools had catered for children and young people who were ordered to be sent their by the courts. These schools provided a general education, with considerable emphasis on the development of vocational skills, and also focused on social readjustment. In 1971, all the functions of the approved schools, including the provision of education, were transferred to local authority social work departments under the terms of the Social Work (Scotland) Act 1968. The institutions were renamed List D schools.

Children with profound and complex learning difficulties were also poorly educated. From 1947, children described as 'ineducable but trainable' were placed in junior occupational centres where they were trained by instructors. Following the Report of the Melville Committee and the provisions of the Education (Mentally Handicapped Children) (Scotland) Act 1974, the centres were renamed schools and teachers were appointed in addition to instructors. The 1974 Act also gave local authorities responsibility for the education of children described as 'ineducable and untrainable'.

The Warnock and HMI reports of 1978
The Warnock report (DES, 1978) has been seen as a watershed in thinking about provision for disabled children. Before 1978, children were 'ascertained' by medical officers as in need of 'special educational treatment' if they were deemed to fit into one of the nine legal categories of 'handicap' described above. There was growing dissatisfaction with the medical view of a fixed 'disability of mind and body' and the Warnock report suggested a new and all-embracing category of 'special educational needs' to replace the former statutory categories of handicap. Whilst recognising that about 20% of children experienced learning difficulties at some time during their education, Warnock suggested that the 2% of children with the most significant difficulties should be assessed by a multi-disciplinary team and their special educational needs recorded formally, along with a legally binding statement by the authority of how it intended to address these needs. These recommendations were incorporated into the Education (Scotland)

Act 1980. The formal document was called the record of needs in Scotland and its English equivalent was termed the statement of needs.

The report published by Scottish HMI entitled *The Education of Pupils with Learning Difficulties in Primary and Secondary Schools* (SED, 1978) questioned the received wisdom concerning the nature and origins of learning difficulties and what schools should do to help children who were experiencing such problems. HM Inspectorate were highly critical of the permanent segregation of lower achieving children within mainstream schools. Such children should be educated alongside their peers but rather than expecting the child to accommodate to a curriculum which might be too difficult or to teaching methods geared to the average child, the onus should be on the mainstream teacher, assisted by the newly-styled learning support teacher, to accommodate the needs of each child. This should be done through the use of differentiated teaching materials and appropriate pedagogy. Looking at the proposals in some detail, it was argued that the focus of remedial education on 'basic skills and numeracy' was too limited. The concept should be broadened to include 'a wider and more diverse range of pupils including those who have trouble coping with these ideas and concepts . . . [and those] whose problems are the result of discontinuity . . . [i.e.] frequent absence or change of school (para 4.2). HM Inspectorate were also critical of the diagnostic techniques used (paras 4.4 and 4.5). Identification and assessment of learning difficulties was seen as too dependent on standardised tests of basic reading and number, as establishing 'the point of onset of difficulty' or uncovering 'deeper problems' (not necessarily educational) which could be the cause of poor performance on basic skills tests, leading to 'adverse effects on [pupils'] whole attitude to school'. The curriculum offered to pupils with learning difficulties was regarded as fundamentally flawed by HMI and new goals were delineated (paras 4.6 to 4.9). These included the following:

- curriculum aims should be the same for all pupils;
- pupils should not all have to study the same things, at the same pace, in the same way;
- objectives for pupils should take into account their age, aptitude and ability;
- the curriculum must sustain skill and interest and get pupils across the 'plateau of learning';
- demands on pupils for higher skill and interest must be not only appropriate but also sufficiently challenging
- de-contextualised activity, such as routine drilling, should be avoided;
- reducing or dropping aspects of the curriculum for individual pupils who require greater provision for the development of basic skills should not be at the expense of enjoyable or creative activities, or those which offer experience of success. (Allan, Brown and Munn (1991).

In relation to pedagogy (para 4.10), an increase in 'discussion' and a combination of class, group and individual methods for both secondary and primary schools were called for. Rather than undertaking separate work with children experiencing difficulty in learning, the emphasis should be on the preparation of differentiated learning materials. In general, HMI recommended less use of whole class teaching and more use of group and individual work. This is in interesting contrast with recent pronouncements by Scotttish HMI (SOEID, 1996a) which, in the light of Scotland's relatively poor showing in International League Tables, suggest that there should be a return to more direct teaching, possibly in the form of whole class teaching. These more recent shifts in policy are discussed in more detail in a later section.

The key to rethinking provision for children with learning difficulties, HMI decided, was to refashion the role of the learning support teacher and her relationship to the mainstream teacher. The following four main roles for the former were indicated:

- acting as a consultant to staff and members of the school management team;
- in co-operation with class and subject teachers offering tutorial support and supportive help in their normal classes to pupils with learning difficulties in any areas of the curriculum;
- providing personal tuition and support for pupils with severe learning difficulties in the process of communication and computation; and
- providing, arranging for or contributing to special services within the school.

A firm message to mainstream teachers, however, was that children with learning difficulties should not be seen as the sole responsibility of the learning support teacher, but primarily of the mainstream class teacher who would draw on the remedial teacher's knowledge and expertise without passing over ultimate responsibility. Despite this shared responsibility, the role of the learning support teacher was couched in extremely wide terms. Elaborating on the four main roles identified above, HMI indicated that the learning support teacher should carry out a number of other tasks including initiating and contributing to staff development; offering a haven for pupils with 'temporary emotional upsets' and for pupils being phased back into mainstream school after a period in residential or special schools; offering a facility in the school whereby pupils can be observed and assessed for a short but intensive period; and offering special expertise in the use of micro-technology, information technology, particularly in relation to differentiation of the curriculum and the analysis and adaptation of published schemes. From their lowly origins as teachers of backward pupils, it appeared that learning support teachers were being urged to adopt one of the most challenging roles in the school. Recognising opportunities for the expansion of this market, colleges of education in Scotland (now incorporated into universities) upgraded their in-service training programmes, offering courses at certificate, diploma and masters levels. Nonetheless, many teachers who adopted the mantle of learning support expert in school continued to lack a specialist qualification and questions remained as to whether they possessed the necessary power and authority to bring about radical change in school.

Conclusion

This chapter traced the early development of provision for children with SEN in Scotland. Always lagging behind developments in mainstream schooling, education for children with SEN was relatively late to develop. Provision for children with sensory impairments developed most rapidly, with schooling for children with complex difficulties lagging far behind. It was not until the mid-1970s that responsibility for the latter group was transferred to education from health. Additional resources were often allocated to children with SEN in the form of smaller class sizes. On the other hand, stigma also accompanied the diagnosis of a need for 'special educational treatment'. The development of schooling for this group of children was informed by both philanthropic concerns, seeing education as a social good in itself, and human capital considerations, suggesting that training for low level employment was preferable to the expectation of a life of idleness. The reports of the Warnock Committee and Scottish HMI were ground-breaking in shifting the emphasis from identifying the child's difficulties to focusing on how the school environment could be modified to allow much higher levels of inclusion. These themes are developed further in subsequent chapters.

CHAPTER 2

JUSTICE IN SPECIAL EDUCATIONAL NEEDS ASSESSMENTS: SOME SCOTTISH/ENGLISH COMPARISONS

Introduction
The Education (Scotland) Act 1980 (as amended), which implemented many of the Warnock Committee's recommendations, was a product of the social democratic political agenda of the 1970s. It was implemented, however, in the very different political climate of the 1980s and 1990s, where the major concern was to increase efficiency and effectiveness by introducing the disciplines of the market into the public sector. In this chapter, the development of special needs provision in the 1990s is described, and is contrasted with developments over the same period in England. The chapter begins with a discussion of competing social policy frameworks and the type of procedural justice which they afford. Drawing on a number of earlier studies (Kirp, 1982; Mashaw,1983; Adler and Sainsbury, 1991, Adler, 2001) and findings from a recent ESRC-funded research project (Riddell et al, 2000; 2002), recent special educational needs policy in Scotland and England is compared. The argument for making comparisons across different countries in the UK is that policy nuances may be thrown into high relief when contrasted with each other (Adler, 1997).

A note on research methods
During the course of the ESRC funded project *Justice Inherent in the Assessment of Special Educational Needs in Scotland and England*, conducted between 1997 and 2000, official policy texts were analysed, interviews conducted with eighteen key informants and questionnaires administered to all local authorities in Scotland and England. On the basis of our preliminary analysis, we chose four case study authorities, two in Scotland and two in England. These differed in relation to their use of mainstream schools to educate children with SEN and also in relation to their rate of appeals. Fifty nine case studies were conducted with families involved in the process of opening a record or statement of needs. In selecting case studies, efforts were made to include children with a range of difficulties and to maintain a balance between 'contested' and 'non-contested' cases. Case studies consisted of interviews with parents, professionals, education officers and, where appropriate, the child. Some meetings between parents and professionals were observed. In the two English authorities, 120 interviews and six observations wee conducted and in the two Scottish authorities, 74

Table 1: Six Normative Models of Administrative Justice

Model	Mode of Decision Making	Legitimating Goal	Mode of Accountability	Characteristic Remedy for User
Bureaucracy	Applying rules	Accuracy	Hierarchical	Administrative review
Professional-ism	Applying knowledge	Public service	Interpersonal	Second opinion: complaint to a professional body
Legality	Weighing-up arguments	Fairness	Independent	Appeal to a court or tribunal (public law)
Managerialism	Managerial autonomy	Efficiency gains	Performance measures	Management sanctions Complaint to ombudsman
Consumersism	Active participation	Consumer satisfaction	Consumer charters	'Voice' and/or compensation through Charter
Markets	Price mechanism	Private sector-profit Public sector-efficiency	Commercial viability	'Exit' and/or course action (private law)

interviews and 9 observations were conducted. Interviews were tape-recorded and transcribed before a thematic analysis was conducted. Finally, a long 'pen portrait' was written for each family. Data from this project are drawn upon in this chapter and the following one.

Special educational needs and competing policy frameworks
The following special educational needs policy analysis draws on the work of a number of commentators including Kirp (1982) and Mashaw (1983). Kirp suggested that 'the way in which a policy problem gets defined says a great deal about how it will be resolved'. Policy frameworks co-exist with each other in a state of dynamic tension:

> They are pursued by different policy actors for different reasons. They have distinctive potentialities and equally distinctive pathologies, and tend to fall in and out of favour with policy-makers over time. Choosing among these policy frameworks affects the policy system and, vitally, the supposed beneficiaries. (Kirp, 1982: 138)

As illustrated in Table 1, each policy framework is characterised by specific forms of decision-making, legitimating goal, nature of accountability and characteristic remedy. The first three policy frameworks in Table 1 were those which have dominated the field of SEN until very recently. Bureaucracy uses rules as the basis for decision-making. It promises accuracy and consistency, is hierarchical and if there is evidence of malfunction then administrative review is the remedy which is likely to be applied. The professional policy framework operates by applying professional judgement, it seeks legitimacy through claiming to place the client's interests above those of the practitioner, accountability is to clients and other professionals and if there is dissatisfaction then a client may complain to a professional body. A policy framework based on legal principles weighs up arguments to determine fair outcomes, which offer it legitimacy. It claims to be independent (hence the depiction of Justice as blind) and appeal is to a court or tribunal.

Other frameworks, specifically managerialism, consumerism and markets, became increasingly important during the 1990s, particularly in England (see below for further discussion). Managerialism refers to new attempts to regulate public services with a view to increasing efficiency, effectiveness and value for money (Clarke and Newman, 1997). To achieve efficiency gains, performance measures are used to assess whether individuals and services have attained pre-specified outcomes. If targets are not met, management sanctions may be applied, which are likely to involve financial penalties or the loss of contracts. Dissatisfied users may complain to the ombudsman. Consumerism, which flourished in the 1990s, was based on the view that service users should have the major say in the nature and delivery of public services. Citizenship was seen increasingly in terms of individual members of the public adopting the role of critical consumer. Consumer charters were intended to provide information on the nature and quality of services people had a right to expect. Individuals were allowed to shape services through exercising 'voice'. Complaints procedures had to be in place and compensation paid to those who had a legitimate grievance with regard to service quality. Finally, markets were seen by the New Right as the ultimate means of raising standards and achieving better value for money. People were increasingly given the power to choose between existing services. Those which were more popular were expected to expand and flourish, whilst unpopular services were intended to wither and die. The mode of accountability within this version of procedural justice is commercial viability and the characteristic remedy for those dissatisfied with services is to exercise their power of exit by choosing a different service.

Policy issues are not usually expressed in terms of a single policy framework; indeed they are more commonly described in terms of composite policy frameworks. Interest groups may suggest that their perspective reflects superior values to those of other contenders, but in practice policy frameworks have different strengths and weaknesses and trade-offs are made between them. Thus, for example, the professional policy framework emphasises service and the need to provide individual solutions to particular problems, but provides few opportunities for legal recourse if the service user disagrees with the professional's perception of the problem. A policy framework based on legality promises to judge individual claims for resources fairly, but the negative trade-off might be that parents who are poor and inarticulate may not be in a position to claim their rights. Such a policy framework has no concern for systemic equity and collective justice. A bureaucratic policy framework might score highly on sticking to agreed procedures, but may be inflexible and unable to meet individual needs. Kirp's analysis thus makes clear that establishing the dominance of a policy framework is a highly political activity, since proponents of different frameworks are in competition with each other.

In the following paragraphs, we explore the development of SEN policy frameworks in Scotland and England in the post-Warnock decades, and in Chapter 3 we explore the implementation of national policies at local level.

Special Educational Needs Policy and Change in Scotland
Following the Education (Scotland) Act 1980 (as amended), SEN policy in Scotland developed relatively slowly for two decades and reflected elements of bureaucracy, professionalism and legality. Under the 1980 Act, authorities had a duty to secure adequate and efficient provision of school education for their area, including adequate and efficient provision for special educational needs. They were required to establish which children belonging to their area, who were 2 years of age or over but under school leaving age, had pronounced, specific or complex special educational needs which required continuing review. They had a duty to open and keep a record of needs for any child who, following assessment, was found to have such needs. Education authorities were also able, but not obliged, to open a record of needs for children under the age of 2. Parents had a duty to ensure that their children of school age received efficient education suitable for their age, aptitude and ability either by sending them to a school under the management of an education authority or by other means.

If parents believed that local authorities were failing in their duty to provide adequate and efficient education, then they had a right of appeal under Section 70 of the Education (Scotland) Act 1980. Dissatisfaction with the process of recording might also result in an appeal to the Secretary of State or, after devolution, Scottish Ministers. The six areas which were open to appeal were the following: the local authority's decision not to open a record or discontinue it after review; the local authority's decision to open a record or continue it after review; the content of Part 3b of the record (summary of the child's impairments); the contents of Part 4 of the record (statement of the child's special educational needs); the content of Part 6 (school placement); and refusal of a placing request. Appeals in relation to school placement were to the Education Appeal Committee run by the local authority and appeals against this committee's decision were made to the Sheriff Court. Appeals in relation to the record were made to

Scottish Ministers. Furthermore, complaints of maladministration could be made to the Ombudsman.

Following the 1980 legislation, it appears that SEN policy in Scotland was influenced by bureaucracy, profession and legal policy frameworks. Rules were laid out pertaining to assessment and recording, such as the requirement for multi-professional assessment and statutory letters. A key role was allocated to professionals in deciding which children merited assessment and the type of provision which was likely to meet their needs. Finally, legality was evident in the specification of avenues for appeal. However, when we look more closely at the SEN policy framework in Scotland in the 1980s and 1990s, it is evident that the professional policy framework dominated and below we explore this in more detail.

It is interesting to note that, compared with England, where a *Code of Practice* with quasi-legal status was introduced in 1994 (DfE, 1994a), no such instrument existed in Scotland. Circular 4/96 (SOEID, 1996) and the *Manual of Good Practice* (SOEID, 1998a) provided guidance on good practice and were much less prescriptive. Circular 4/96, for example, emphasised the need for flexible approaches to recording reflecting circumstances in local authorities rather than fixed and consistent national policies. There was no attempt to specify in detail which children should receive a record of needs, and this led to variable local practices (see Chapter 4 which deals with evidence on inclusion). Although statutory assessment procedures were tightly specified (SOEID, 1996) the school-based stages of assessment were left to the school's discretion. There was no requirement to have a register of all children with SEN and no regulatory provision for review of children who had SEN but were not recorded. Whilst it might have been expected that the looser criteria for recording in Scotland compared with statementing in England would lead to more records of need being opened, in fact the reverse was true (In 2000, about 2% of Scottish school-aged children had records of need compared with 3% of English children). This suggests that Scottish professionals used the fluidity of the system to resist inflationary pressures on recording. English parents, on the other hand, used the emerging consumerist policy framework to push for greater resources reflected in higher rates of statementing.

In addition to recording criteria, in Scotland many procedural matters were relatively loosely defined. For example, Circular 4/96 stipulated that the period between notification by the authority that an assessment might be necessary through to the opening of the record should not exceed 6 months. However, although Circular 4/96 suggested: '. . . it is good practice and courteous if the reasons for this can be promptly explained to parents', no penalties were incurred by LEAs where delays occurred. The Accounts Commission for Scotland (Accounts Commission for Scotland, 2002) noted that the average time taken for assessment was 28 weeks. However, this masked wide variation, with six councils taking on average less than 20 weeks. Slightly less than 10% of assessments took more than a year to complete, while three councils reported that more than 25% of their assessments took longer than a year to complete. Compared with data published two years earlier, it appeared that assessments were being completed more rapidly.

In England, as we shall see below, greater efforts have been made to empower parents, leading to a consumerist approach in some local authorities (see Chapter 3). In Scotland, fewer efforts have been made to involve parents. The Scottish Office published the document *A Parents Guide to Special Educational Needs* in 1993, equivalent to the DfE's parental guide of 1994 (DfE, 1994b). The guide emphasised the importance of flexibility at local levels for professionals to decide on appropriate forms of provision and dealt with appeals in a fairly cursory manner. The fact that, in Scotland, parents had no right of appeal against the provisions stipulated in the record was glossed over and the document failed to mention the possibility of making a complaint of maladministration to the ombudsman. This might explain why no complaint involving the assessment of special educational needs has ever been the subject of a formal investigation by the ombudsman in Scotland. In contrast, the annual number of reports involving SEN issued by the CLA in England was as follows: 1994/95–24, 1995/96–53, 1996/97–42, 1997/87–19, 1998/99–20. In addition to the lack of specificity of the record compared with the statement of needs, the major difference between Scotland and England in relation to SEN has been the lack of a robust appeals system. Parents have been deterred from appealing to Scottish Ministers because the system has been lengthy and secretive. The fact that it was not possible to appeal in relation to the content of the record also made the system less meaningful. The more radical approach of the Special Educational Needs Tribunal (SENT) in England is discussed below.

Since the advent of the Scottish Parliament in 1997, there is evidence that the policy stasis of the 1980s and 1990s has shifted, with much greater discussion and implementation of new policies. For example, the Standards in Scotland's Schools etc. (Scotland) Act 2000 established a presumption that all children would be educated in mainstream schools. Exceptionally, children might be educated elsewhere if one or more of these circumstances apply to education in a mainstream school:

• it would not be suitable to a child's ability or aptitude;
• it would not be compatible with the provision of efficient education for other children;
• it would result in unreasonable public expenditure that would not ordinarily occur.

A child could still be educated in a mainstream school even if such exceptional circumstances occurred, but the wishes of the child and parents must be taken into account. This legislation, in terms of underscoring the expectation of mainstream placement, is backed up by draft legislation on planning for pupils with SEN. The Education (Disability Strategies and

Pupils' Records) (Scotland) Bill, published in 2001, proposes to place additional duties on educational providers to produce accessibility strategies, indicating their plans to make both the curriculum and the built environment accessible to all children. The draft bill complements and support the requirements of the Disability Discrimination Act as amended by the Special Educational Needs and Disability Act 2001, which is discussed more fully in Chapter 6.

There has also been far greater emphasis on the development of systems to encourage joined-up government and social inclusion. The report *For Scotland's Children* (Scottish Executive, 2001a) explores key issues with regard to the integration of children's services in Scotland. A number of important recommendations are made, including the development of shared financial approaches between health and education, the development of a modular information and assessment format and the appointment of a Children's Commissioner. The rapidity of recent policy development suggests that, after a period of little change, radical innovations are likely in the sphere of SEN over the next decade as new solutions are sought to including children with SEN in the educational mainstream.

Finally, following the publication of the *Report on the Inquiry into Special Educational Needs* (Scottish Parliament Education, Culture and Sports Committee, 2001), the Scottish Executive published a consultation document on assessment and recording (Scottish Executive, 2001b). The Government's response to the Consultation (Scottish Executive, 2001) put forward a number of suggestions for systemic reform. Whilst most children's needs would be identified by routine progress monitoring arrangements, education authorities would be required to have a staged intervention process in place for children requiring additional support. This process would include children for whom English is an additional language, refugees and asylum seekers, children with social, emotional and behavioural difficulties and gypsy/traveller children. It might also include gifted or more able children. The legal underpinning for this measure would come from section 2 of the Standards in Scotland's Schools etc. Act 2000, which states that education authorities have a duty to secure education directed to the full development of the personality, talents and mental and physical abilities of the child. The planned intervention process would build on and expand information recorded within Personal Learning Plans and Individualised Education Programmes. The record of needs would be replaced with a Co-ordinated Support Plan (CSP) for children with complex educational needs, such as require continuing review. The Plan would normally be provided when it is clear that the mainstream school or nursery which the child is attending cannot meet his/her needs out of its existing resources. There is a lack of clarity about whether children with complex needs in special schools will have a CSP. It will not be compulsory for a child being assessed with a view to opening a CSP to have both medical and psychological assessments, but these would always be undertaken if requested by the parent. A particularly radical proposal is that each local authority or group of authorities has in place a mediation service, and that an independent Tribunal be established to hear appeals. It is proposed that both parents and children have the right of appeal to the Tribunal against any part of the CSP, and an education authority's decision to open or discontinue such a plan.

To summarise, whilst policy frameworks rooted in bureaucracy, profession and legal system were all evident in Scottish SEN policy in the 1980s and 1990s, professionalism was the dominant framework. Positive trade-offs included an emphasis on meeting the needs of the child and the family in a flexible way. Negative trade-offs were a lack of concern for parents' and children's rights and a lack of consistency in policy implementation. The recent consultation paper on assessment and recording and the government's response indicates a move towards legality and consumerism, with local authorities having a duty to provide parents with better information and allowing them enhanced rights of appeal.

Special Educational Needs Policy and Change in England
SEN policy in England in the 1980s, as in Scotland, reflected a balance between the traditional forms of procedural justice based on bureaucracy, professionalism and the legal system. Under the terms of the 1993 Education Act, a number of significant changes took place, increasingly reflecting the wider agenda of marketisation, managerialism and consumerism within the public sector. Parents' organisations in England, arguably stronger than their Scottish counterparts, played an active role in driving reforms. It was believed that some local authorities were failing to put enough funding into the education of children with SEN, and as a result voluntary organisations, including the Council for Disabled Children, campaigned for a tighter legal framework. The 1993 Education Act in England required the Secretary of State to publish a Code of Practice to regulate the assessment and statementing of children with SEN. From September 1994, all state schools were obliged to have regard to the *Code of Practice on the Identification and Assessment of Special Educational Needs* (DfE, 1994b) and publish information about their policies for children with special educational needs. Each school's governing body had to include a named individual with particular responsibility for special educational needs provision.

The Code of Practice's requirements necessitated the identification of a Special Educational Needs Co-ordinator or co-ordinating team in each school and in many schools a new appointment had to be made. The role of the SENCO was to implement the school-based stages of assessment and to co-ordinate reviews for all children with SEN. The Code laid down very strict time lines for the completion of the various stages of assessment and statementing, the entire process taking less than seven months, with a particularly tight two week period allowed for the drafting of the statement. Illness of local education authority staff was not regarded as sufficient excuse for non-completion, although illness or bereavement of the family would count as a good reason for delay. The Commission for Local Administration in England published data on average assessment times in each local authority, and failure to comply with these timescales might justify a complaint of maladministration being lodged with the ombudsman (DfE, 1994b).

In addition to describing how assessment and statementing should be conducted, the Code also specified criteria for triggering assessment and opening a statement in relation to the following categories: learning difficulties, specific learning difficulties (for example dyslexia), emotional and behavioural difficulties, physical disabilities, hearing impairments, visual impairments, speech and language difficulties, and medical conditions. This might be interpreted as a move away from the anti-labelling approach advocated by Warnock in favour of a recognition of types of impairment and attendant educational difficulties.

The 1993 Education Act also established a parent's right to take a case to a Special Educational Needs Tribunal (SENT), set up in 1994 and hearing its first cases in 1995. The aim of the SENT was to act as final arbiter where consensus had broken down between parent and the local education authority. Each year since its inception, there has been an increase in the number of appeals referred to the SENT and these were unevenly distributed throughout the country. London boroughs had the highest rates of appeal, at around 4.5% per 10,000 pupils (Special Educational Needs Tribunal, 2000). There were also relatively high rates of appeal in the south east and pockets in the north-west.

Parents were able to appeal to the SENT with regard to the nominated school or the level of resources specified on the statement of needs. Legal representation was used by about 11% of parents and 14% of parents made use of lay representation, often provided by the Independent Panel for Special Educational Advice (IPSEA) or a voluntary organisation such as the British Dyslexia Association. Legal aid was not available to individuals bringing cases to the SENT. About a third of parents presented independent assessments as evidence to the Tribunal and these appeared to influence the outcome of the appeal in favour of the parent (Harris, 1997). The advent of the Special Educational Needs Tribunal was indicative of the growing importance of the legal and consumerist policy frameworks in England, with individual parents empowered to seek justice from an impartial body.

Recognising the danger that a rapid swing towards a legal policy framework might lead to escalating and unmanageable costs, the DfEE included an element within the Grants for Education, Support and Training (GEST) programme, initially for three years and subsequently extended, to fund the development of Parent Partnership Schemes. The main objectives of the programme were to encourage active partnership between parents and professionals with a view to minimising conflict and reducing the number of statutory SEN appeals (Wolfendale and Cook, 1997).

To summarise, in England during the 1990s the traditional frameworks of bureaucracy, professionalism and legality persisted. However, there was a grater emphasis on legality through the establishment of the SENT. New frameworks were also introduced. Managerialism was evident in the regulation of the performance of schools and local authorities through the Code of Practice. Performance indicators were used to specify and monitor desirable outcomes. Consumerism was also increasingly in evidence, with parents being actively encouraged to take a more active role in the process of assessment and statementing, and to appeal if dissatisfied. Local authorities were obliged to make parents aware of the choice of school and other types of provision available to them, encouraging the operation of a market in the field of SEN with parents, at least in theory, having more opportunity for choice and control over services.

Shifting policy frameworks had both positive and negative trade-offs. The greater emphasis on consumerism, legality and markets meant that parents were able to exert more control over the services on offer. However, this produced a number of pressures within the system. The Green Paper *Excellence for All Children: Meeting Special Educational Needs* (DfEE, 1997) drew attention to the rapid acceleration in the number of children with statements in mainstream primary and secondary schools and the pressure on resources which this produced. It was suggested that the number of statements should be reduced and ultimately the system should be scrapped, although this produced an outcry from parents' groups and voluntary organisations and was therefore not pursued.

The operation of the Code of Practice in schools has also involved both positive and negative trade-offs. There is evidence that SENCOs have experienced a significant increase in their administrative responsibilities, spend less time with children and are suffering considerable stress (Male and May, 1997). However, their status has risen markedly in the eyes of their colleagues as a result of their new place in the school bureaucracy and their close links with the senior management team and the LEA (Garner, 1996). Senior figures in LEAs have a generally positive view of the Code because of its administrative clarity and its ready fit with bureaucracy and managerialism (Millward and Skidmore, 1998). The negative trade-off, according to Vincent et al (1996), is the growing curtailment of the professional discretion traditionally enjoyed by teachers, educational psychologists and junior LEA officers.

The impact of the SENT in promoting legality and consumerism has also both positive and negative aspects (Harris, 1997; Evans, 1998; 1999). On the positive side, it was seen as non-intimidating, user-friendy and impartial. On the negative side, it was seen as 'a weapon of the middle classes' (Education Officer cited by Evans, 1997) thus undermining the LEAs' attempts to ensure equity of resource allocation. There were also concerns that some parents are much more able than others to adopt the role of the critical consumer, with few appeals being made from people living in socially disadvantaged areas and from minority ethnic families. The promotion by local education authorities of Parent Partnership schemes might be seen as a deliberate attempt to tilt the balance away from legality and consumerism and towards professionalism.

There have been recent signs of some changes of direction in England. The revised Code of Practice (DfES, 2001) cut down on regulation, reducing the process of assessment to only two stages. In addition, it required authorities to 'set out' rather than 'specify' the provision to be made to meet children's special educational needs. Resources to purchase additional classroom assistants were given directly to schools, with no guarantee that they would be used for this purpose. The number of appeals to the SENT continued to rise, and in 1999/000 2,463 were registered, an increase of just over 2% on the previous year (Special Educational Needs Tribunal Annual Report, 1999-2000 (DfEE, 2000).

Conclusion

Having summarised key policy documents of the 1990s and reviewed evidence of their impact, it is appropriate to consider how SEN policy in England and Scotland may be understood in terms of the policy frameworks outlined earlier. In Scotland in the 1990s, the professional policy framework, backed up by bureaucracy and, to a lesser extent, legality, continued to hold sway and the language of official documents warned parents that although they might act as partners, final decisions on service provision still lay with professionals. The system was relatively unregulated, with no management sanction for time delays in conducting assessments. Educational psychologists retained considerable freedom in deciding which individuals and groups of children were to receive records. Schools did not automatically register all children with SEN and school-based stages of assessment, whilst recommended, were not uniformly applied. Appeals mechanisms were time-consuming, complicated and lacked independence.

In England, a wider repertoire of policy frameworks appears to have been in play, with elements of bureaucracy, professionalism, legality, managerialisnm, consumerism and marketisation all in evidence. The tighter regulation of assessment and statementing was promoted by voluntary organisations and welcomed by civil servants and senior administrators who saw them as a way of managing the system more effectively and curbing the discretion of less senior officers, educational psychologists and teachers. According to Harris (1997), lawyers also welcomed the changes, recognising education as a fruitful field for future work. Hostility towards tighter regulation was expressed most strongly by 'street level bureaucrats' (Weatherley and Lipsky, 1977; Lipsky, 1980; Vincent et al, 1996) such as SENCOs, educational psychologists and education officers, who have responsibility for implementation but little control over the conditions within which this takes place. Moves towards a wider policy repertoire also produced both positive and negative trade-offs for parents. Bowers and

Wilkinson (1998) noted that some parents disliked being part of a tightly rule-bound system, where they were required to respond to communications from the Local Education Authority within strictly specified periods. Some parents were also opposed to the compulsory registration of children with SEN and their regular review, which might be seen as a disciplinary rather than benign mechanism. On the positive side, many parents and voluntary organisations welcomed a more tightly controlled system allowing a greater degree of parental choice and with an inbuilt system of legal redress. A negative trade-off of policy frameworks built on consumerism, legality and the market was the lack of equal access to procedural justice, since there is considerable evidence that socially advantaged parents are in a much better position to act as critical consumers.

In both Scotland and England, the winds of change have been blowing and recently the SEN policy frameworks of the two countries appear to have been converging. The Scottish Executive response to the consultation on the future of assessment and recording in Scotland suggested that the dominance of professionalism may be giving way to a wider range of policy frameworks. Procedural justice, it appears, will in the future, be informed by a wider range of policy models, although the final shape of emerging SEN policy is, at the time of writing, unclear. Educational psychologists have already indicated their lack of enthusiasm for the proposed SEN Tribunal which would, in their view, give too much voice to the consumer and increase dissent. In England, the revised Code indicates a desire to return a greater degree of power to professionals, particularly those working in schools, to decide on the distribution of resources to children with SEN. Again, the outcome of this new policy direction is unknown and is certain to be challenged by those seeking to protect the rights of parents and children. A further important unifying measure is the extension of the Disability Discrimination Act 1995 to education. This new legislation covers Scotland, England and Wales and indicates a shift away from the professional assessment of needs as the basis for resource distribution. In the future, resource distribution will be based on what is required to allow disabled children and young people to exercise their right to full social inclusion. The implications of the legislation are discussed further in Chapter 6.

CHAPTER 3

SPECIAL EDUCATIONAL NEEDS AND JUSTICE IN PRACTICE: SOME LOCAL AUTHORITY CASE STUDIES

Introduction

In Chapter 2, the policy frameworks underpinning post-war SEN policy were described. It was noted that until relatively recently, the dominant frameworks were based on professionalism, bureaucracy and legality. In England during the 1980s and 90s, there was a growth in the influence of different policy frameworks based on managerialism, consumerism and markets. Whilst these elements were also present in Scotland, professionalism remained the dominant influence. Systems in both England and Scotland are undergoing change at the moment, with a growing emphasis in both countries on mixed economies of welfare. The White Paper *Modernising Government* (Cabinet Office, 1999) stated a commitment to the development of public services which were of high quality and efficient, "joined up" and strategic and focused on public service users, not the interests of providers. The documents envisaged a mixed economy of service delivery, with an emphasis on service outcomes. These goals are obviously in line with the further development of managerialism, markets and consumerism across the public sector.

So far the discussion has focused on the broad thrust of public policy at national level. However, in translating policies from the statute book to the local level, there are many opportunities for subversion and transformation as local actors interpret and recreate these policies. This chapter describes the implementation of national policies in four local authorities, two in Scotland and two in England. Like Chapter 2, it draws on research carried out as part of an ESRC project (Riddell et al, 2001) between 1997 and 2000. Having identified some broad differences between Scottish and English policies, our aim was to explore the extent to which these global differences could still be discerned at local level. The four local authorities are explored in relation to the six policy frameworks set out in Table 1. Following the interviews with key informants and the local authority questionnaire survey, case study authorities were selected which appeared to exemplify a particular policy framework. However, in-depth discussion with local policy-makers and parents indicated a more complex picture than had been anticipated. Below, each local authority, and its position within our policy typology, is described.

Local Authority 1 : Bureaucratised professionalism

Local Authority 1 was a Scottish city which had experienced a long period of industrial decline. Forty two per cent of the city's population lived in an area of deprivation. In fifty four per cent of city schools, more than half the children were entitled to free school meals. The city had an unemployment rate of 11.6%, the highest of any council area in Scotland and 29% above the UK level. More than forty per cent of children in the city were in families dependent on income support. The city had a high and increasing number of single parent households and a relatively high minority ethnic population.

There were a number of government schemes and plans geared towards addressing problems of poverty and social exclusion. These included a number of Social Inclusion Partnerships, a Healthy Cities Development Plan and a Health Improvement Plan. Due to a major building programme in the 1950s and 60s, the authority had a great deal of special school provision (31 special schools and three special units attached to mainstream) and as a result 82% of children with records of need were in special schools. Despite the fact that it did not record children with social, emotional and behavioural difficulties, the authority had a relatively high proportion of recorded children, reflecting high levels of social deprivation in the area. The key policy features of Local Authority 1 are summarised in Table 2.

Practice in this authority was not always in line with the Scottish Executive's *Manual of Good Practice*. For instance, the Scottish Executive advised that parents should be invited to attend all statutory assessments, but case study parents were only routinely invited to attend the medical assessment. Assessment reports were distributed when requested, but parents had not always seen these prior to case conferences, which made it difficult for them to question professional judgements. At the start of the statutory assessment, parents were given some written information on procedures, but this tended to downplay the legal significance of the record and parents' right of appeal. The Named Person was described as 'someone to whom you can talk and can help you' instead of a technical adviser and advocate as in Scottish Executive guidance. Only one parent in our case studies within this authority used a Named Person as an advocate. The statutory letters issued within this local authority tended to be legalistic in tone, and the recommended timescale for the opening of a record was not mentioned.

In this authority, the high level of expenditure on special educational needs was of major concern. Educational psychologists were instructed to write the record in general terms without committing the authority to any specific expenditure. Educational psychologists in the authority found themselves pulled in different directions by the conflicting expectations that they could both act as honest brokers giving parents the best possible advice about their children's needs, but also as agents of the authority, chairing the meetings and drafting the record in terms of the resources available to the authority. One educational psychologist suggested that the record of needs was not a productive document because of its generality

Table 2: Model Features of Scottish Local Authority 1

Models	Features	
BUREAUCRACY	Education Authority stipulates particular phrases to be used where extra resources are implicated, EA also edits final copy of Record. EPs see themselves as working on behalf of the Education Authority but often resentful of their professional status being compromised. Co-incidence of interest between EPs and education officers	NB: EP in sole charge of bureaucratic process until draft RoN stage when local authority sends copies to parents and other professionals prior to sending final version of RoN.
PROFESSION-ALISM	EPs generally perceived to have most influence — have absolute control over RoN process and outcome Decision to commence assessments with regard to opening a RoN made by EP. Parents, schools and other professionals can initiate recording but this rarely happens. On completion of assessments EP recommends to Senior Education Officer if RoN should be opened. EP's decision rarely if ever questioned.	NB: EPs hold vital gate-keeping role with regard to commencing assessments leading to RoN. EPs conscious of privileged position in RoN process — best qualified to guide the process.
LEGALITY	Parents may object to school nominated on the RoN, but little understanding of the process or their power within it.	NB:Parents unaware of the potential of the RoN document to challenge the EA. Knowledge of process restricted to EP's explanation and 2 page description. Procedures within EA Appeal Committee seriously flawed. No data available on SEN placement appeals or appeals to Scottish ministers.
MANAGERIA-LISM	Accounts Commission for Scotland publishes information of time taken to open Record. No other PIs published nationally.	NB: EA takes much longer to open Record than 6 months recommended time.

CONSUMERISM	Little local support available to parents. ISEA offers advice to parents on SEN procedures and rights	NB: Few opportunities for parents to exercise 'voice'. Sparse information available. System not 'user friendly'. Named Person little used — often presented to parents by EP as next of kin or family friend rather than advocate.
MARKETS	Information not routinely provided on possible schools.	

and another spoke of 'the raging ambiguity of our position' because of the requirement to act as an agent of the authority whilst serving the child's best interests.

Parents were somewhat confused about the purpose of the record and their role within the process. One parent explained that she became so disillusioned with the record of needs that she did not bother to read the final document. Views like this were typically seen by educational psychologists as evidence that the process was too bureaucratic and difficult for parents to understand.

To summarise, the policy framework operating in Local Authority 1 may be characterised as an example of bureaucratised professionalism. Whilst it was claimed that professionals operated independently of the authority, in reality it appeared that they allied themselves with its interests. Opportunities for parents to act as critical consumers, to choose a school or use their legal rights were limited. Other professionals, such as medical officers, who might raise parental expectations by suggesting alternative views of the child's needs, had only marginal involvement.

Local Authority 2: centralised bureaucracy
Local Authority 2 was a medium sized Scottish authority. It was predominantly rural, with a few small towns. The area had little industry and farming employed increasingly fewer people; tourism was a much bigger employer. There was some rural poverty, with 11.5% of children entitled to free school meals. Because of its rural nature, it was never practical to build special schools (the area had only two) because this would have involved children travelling long distances. Instead, special units attached to mainstream schools, some with specific specialisms, had developed. Sixty nine per cent of recorded children were counted as being in mainstream, although some spent very little or no time in mainstream classes. About 2% of children had records of needs, slightly above the national average.

Table 3: Model Features of Scottish Local Authority 2

Models	Features	
BUREAUCRACY	Head of Psychological and Learning Support Services (HPLS) decides if RoN procedure should commence. Area Managers of Learning Support (AMLS) collate assessments. HPLS personally decides if RoN should be opened. EPs acknowledge conflict between their professional role and role of EA.	NB: EPs initiate RoN process by recommending to HPLS that process commences. AMLS makes final decision. Criteria not written down and decided by panel as in English local authorities.
PROFESSION-ALISM	Based on professional judgement, EPs recommend to HPLS which children should have statutory assessment. EPs perceive themselves as advocates for parents. AMLS has responsibility for SEN procedures and managing SEN budget. Parents, schools and other professionals can initiate statutory assessment but this rarely happens.	NB: EPs hold vital gate-keeping role with regard to commencing assessments leading to a RoN. HPLS however personally views and approves all applications to maintain uniform/ equal treatment for all RoN.
LEGALITY	Parents viewed by EPs and AMLS as important in that they could object to placement named on the RoN and required to be involved in the process. Where dissatisfied parents quick to challenge RoN. EA has highest rate of appeals to Scottish Ministers. No complaints to Ombudsman.	NB: Parents more aware of the potential of the RoN to challenge the local authority than those in EA1. Knowledge of process restricted to brief by EP and accompanying and accompanying literature. Named Person little. EPs often alluded to themselves as advocates for parents in the system.
MANAGERIA-LISM	PIs published on time taken to open RoN.	NB: In 1999/2000, EA had longest average time for opening RoN.
CONSUMERSIM	Some local vol orgs encourage expression of voice – but not V active.	NB: EA makes little attempt to engage parents in process
MARKETS	Parents not given list of schools. Choice restricted by geography – rural area.	NB: Choice of school out-with designated special unit not encouraged. Only 1 special school.

   Local Authority 2 had developed a centralised bureaucratic system for the management of special educational needs as presented in Table 3.

   Some years ago, it was decided that educational psychologists were too closely involved in co-ordinating recording procedures, and this might compromise their position as independent professionals acting on behalf of their client. It was therefore decided to focus the role of the educational psychologist on assessing children's needs and offering advice to schools. The task of orchestrating the recording process was delegated to three area managers, each liasing with a Principal Educational Psychologist and reporting to the Head of Psychological and Learning Support Services (HPLSS).

   In order to achieve fairness and consistency, the HPLSS makes the final decision in all cases on the opening of a record of needs and resource allocation. Before the opening of a record, schools were required to demonstrate that they had implemented the staged process as set out in *A Manual of Good Practice*. This very centralised decision-making process had a marked impact on the role of educational psychologists and the opportunities for parental involvement which are discussed below.

   The approach to recording in the authority was influenced by the view of the HPLSS that the record of needs was a document which had outlived its usefulness. He drew attention to the fact that Circular 4/96 states that the record of needs does not need to quantify provision, and this should be specified in the Individualised Educational Programme (IEP). Research on IEPs (Banks et al, 2001), however, found no examples of provision being specified in these documents. The HPLSS believed that learning support needs in particular schools should be established through an annual audit in which schools report children's additional needs to the authority. The record of needs, in his view, was redundant and simply encouraged some parents to believe that they could extract additional resources from the authority. When parents requested a statutory assessment, they were often told that this was not necessary because provision was already being made for their child as a result of an annual audit of resource needs. This contrasted with the situation in England, where the Code of Practice required the statement of needs to specify all the special educational provision that the LEA considered appropriate for *all* the child's learning difficulties. The statement was also expected to specify the child's non-educational needs and describe the provision to be made by health and other services. Parents were becoming increasingly restive in Local Authority 2 and the authority had the highest number of appeals to Scottish Ministers of any Scottish authority. Because it is not possible to appeal against Part V of the record (the measures proposed by the authority) parents appealed against the description of the child's special educational needs and the authority's decision on whether to open a record.

   When multi-disciplinary meetings were abolished in Local Authority 2 in the mid-1990s, educational psychologists first felt bereft of an important role. Subsequently, they recognised that this enabled them to play a more pro-active part in advocating for the parents or children, a role which would have been compromised if acting primarily for the authority with the SEN budget in mind. Nonetheless, some educational psychologists still felt that they had been somewhat marginalised and would have preferred a greater role, although others believed that they were better able to preserve their professional integrity if they remained at arm's length from the process. Schools also felt that they had been squeezed out of the process and the professional perspectives of headteachers, learning support staff and classroom teachers were no longer required. In response to feelings of both the educational psychologists and parents that they had been marginalised and bureaucratic power had become concentrated at a single point in the system, the HPLSS had recently re-instated the meeting to discuss the terms of the record of needs, although he still considered that this was not the best use of the authority's resources.

To summarise, Scottish Local Authority 2 exemplified a bureaucratic and highly centralised approach, which marginalised the power and input of professionals and parents. This allowed the HPLSS, originally an educational psychologist, to keep a tight handle on issues of budgetary allocation and to oversee the system for consistency. His view of fairness, however, was not audited by any other interest group, and therefore was likely to be somewhat partial. The type of accountability mechanisms rooted in the Code of Practice were absent in both Scottish local authorities. The only public performance indicator was the measure of time taken to open a record of needs published by the Accounts Commission for Scotland. In 1998/99, Local Authority 2 was amongst the slowest in Scotland. Comparing the two Scottish authorities, there were strong similarities in that both were based on a bureaucratic approach and attempted to minimise consumerism and legal frameworks. They were also hostile to mangerialism, because of its threats to their autonomy. Professionals were allowed to exercise some degree of discretion, as long as this did not interfere with the smooth running of the bureaucratic system.

Local Authority 3: Benign bureaucracy
Local Authority 3 was a small metropolitan authority in the heart of an old northern coal field in England serving a relatively homogeneous and largely disadvantaged community. There were few people from minority ethnic backgrounds and a low proportion of people moving into or out of the area. Unemployment in the area was high (12.8% compared with 7.4% nationally). Education had traditionally had a low profile among the aspirations of the community, with a low proportion of students remaining in education after the age of 16 (53% as opposed to 70% nationally). The 1991 census showed that higher education qualifications were held by only 7.5% of the population, compared with a national figure of 13.5%. According to a 1999 OFSTED report, standards in schools were low compared with

national averages and those of similar LEAs. In this report, the authority was criticised for 'having done little to raise the profile of education and levels of pupils' achievements' and was seen as having 'complicated and inefficient internal management arrangements'. Criticisms were also made of its SEN management, and attention was drawn to the fact that in 1997–98 less than 1% of Statements were drawn up within the required timescale. By 1999, this had improved to 51.4%.

In recognition of its high level of social disadvantage and low educational attainments, a number of social inclusion and educational improvement projects were underway. The local authority had Education and Health Action Zones, an Educational Partnership Plan and a School Development and Effectiveness Strategy. Most children were educated in mainstream and the authority had only 3 special schools, 4 units attached to mainstream and 1 stand-alone unit. Slightly less than 2% of the population had Statements and 83% of statemented children were educated in mainstream schools. This high use of mainstream schools was not as a result of a major policy change, but rather because special schools had never been built in this area. Some mainstream schools had been adapted to accommodate pupils with physical disabilities while the units attached offer specialised teaching to children with hearing impairments, specific learning difficulties, autism and behaviour problems. Local Authority 3 had very low rates of appeals to the SENT. According to the Special Educational Needs Tribunal Annual Report, two appeals were registered with the SENT in 1998/99, five in 1997/98 and two in 1998/99. During this period there was one complaint of maladministration to the CLA.

Table 4 summarises some key features of the authority in terms of the policy frameworks described in Table 1. As noted earlier, the national SEN policy and legal framework in England allows parents greater opportunities to operate as service consumers within a marketised system, whilst at the same time tightening the management regime within which professionals operate. Nonetheless, there were elements of all six models in the authority with evident tensions between them.

Many features of policy and procedure in the local authority were geared towards assisting parents to play an active role in the assessment and statementing of their children and to seek legal redress where appropriate. However, as the low rate of appeal suggests, parents were not closely involved in the process. They did not generally seek to use their power of exit to request a placement in a school other than that suggested by the local authority. In the same way, they did not use their voice as consumers to request different forms of support. For example, most statements simply stated that a child would receive a specific number of hours of additional support form a classroom assistant, and parents did not normally request additional support such as speech therapy. Questions arise as to why the provisions of the 1996 Education Act, which promoted consumerism, markets, and legality, had not had a more radical effect on the nature of

Table 4: Model Features of English Local Authority 3

Models	Features	
BUREAUCRACY	Decision on who gets a statutory assessment made by committee. Members:- 8 officers, 2 professionals and 1 administrative assistant. This most important decision. Committee works to criteria when deciding whether to begin a statutory assessment. Decision on who gets a statement (of lesser significance) made by sole officer. Underpinned by system of internal monitoring. Formulaic allocation of EP time to schools.	NB: Most of the members of this committee have been practising teachers. Distinction between officers and professionals is blurred.
PROFESSION-ALISM	EPs generally perceived to have most influence. In some cases MO/ psychiatrist. EPs see themselves as working on behalf of the child.	NB: EPs hold no gatekeeper role when decision made to begin a statutory assessment. EPs stressed they have no more power or influence than any other report writer when decision is made on who gets a statement. EPs valued working in this way.
LEGALITY	Regulations within the Code of Practice give parents clear grounds for appeal/complaint if procedures not followed. Rights to appeal to SENT are set out in the Education Act 1996.	Very low rate of appeal to SENT or complaint to Ombudsman
MANAGERIA-LISM	Performance indicator of time taken to open a Statement of Needs published. Concern to adhere to recommended timescales. Recent OFSTED report recommended more tightly regulated systems to raise standards in schools and to improve administration of SEN, including budegtary control.	NB: Evidence of local authority subjecting systems to tighter scrutiny – research seen as element in this.

CONSUMERISM	If parents make firm representation at the draft statement stage, generally seen to have most power. Parent Partnership Officer seeking to engage with parents.	NB: Few parents informed of their rights beyond the legal minimum. Parents tend to trust professionals to do the right thing. Parents did not indicate they had used LEA initiated pamphlets. Named Person little used. Evidence of heads acting in that capacity or suggesting Named Person not needed, thereby counteracting the independent nature of the role. Schools used this ploy to protect own level of support hours. At the draft statement stage, evidence of some schools using parents to fight for support hours to mean one to one rather than small group hours, even when parents not in agreement.
MARKETS	Parents given list of schools from which to choose .	NB: Choice of school restricted to mainstream because of lack of special schools.

parents' participation. It appeared that, although information about their rights was made available, many parents experienced extreme social disadvantage and were therefore not able to make full use of possible choices. For example, with the initial letter, parents were given a DfEE booklet explaining the process of drawing up a statement. However, many parents interviewed did not find this booklet accessible. For a time, a senior officer had hand-delivered all initial notices of the authority's intention to begin the process of statutory assessment. However, this practice was discontinued because of changes in personnel. It was felt that whilst it had been very worthwhile for some parents in terms of demystifying the process, for others, according to a Senior Officer, it was 'a waste of time because you go and you can tell they're not listening to you'. Instead of providing parents with more help, this officer concluded that there was no point in trying to secure greater involvement because parents lacked understanding and motivation, thus locating the fault with them rather than the system of communication.

It was evident from the case studies conducted that parents under social stress were resistant to becoming involved in the statementing process. Others wished for greater involvement but were uncertain about how this might be achieved.

It was also evident that the managerialist regime associated with the Code of Practice did not work to parents' advantage. Professionals almost always met their targets in terms of completing assessments within the prescribed timescale, but sometimes did this by failing to ensure that parents fully understood the procedures. For example, parents were routinely sent copies of all assessment reports with the draft statement as recommended in the Code, but did not receive them at the same time as the professionals and therefore had a shorter period of time to consult and consider the need for further action (e.g. requesting a second medical opinion). Nobody went through the reports with parents to make sure they were understood. In addition, as required by law, parents were given a list of all the possible schools which their child might attend. However, the local authority almost always recommended that the child should be placed in the local mainstream school, thus closing down rather than opening up discussion of alternatives.

On the face of it, parents in Local Authority 3 were given all the information they needed to use the legal framework, to exercise voice or to use their power of exit to select a different type of school from that nominated by the local authority . They were informed of their right of choice and to appeal, and after the delivery of the draft statement were offered two meetings with a senior official in addition to access to a Parent Partnership Officer. If a resolution was not reached after these meetings, parents were encouraged to begin appeals proceedings. Throughout the process, educational psychologists described themselves operating as independent agents. They provided important advice to the local authority officers, but did not make the final decision on whether to open a statement; nor did they draft the statement itself. Despite this independence, a large number of appeals would undoubtedly have added to the educational psychologists' workload and therefore it was not in their interests to encourage parents to appeal. Whereas parents in more socially advantaged areas were able to form their own support groups, draw on the expertise of the voluntary sector and commission independent assessments, these options were less likely to be available in this authority. Whilst parents did have access to a Parent Partnership Officer whose job was to reconcile parents to the authority's position, very few appointed a Named Person to act as independent advocate. To summarise, whilst the national SEN framework in England emphasised a type of procedural justice based on legality, markets, consumerism and managerialism, elements of post-war bureaucracy and professionalism survived.

Local Authority 4: Consumer-focused managerialism
Local Authority 4 was an inner London borough with a long-standing Conservative administration. The borough contained some very affluent

areas but overall was significantly more disadvantaged than most areas in England. The proportion of pupils eligible for free school meals (31.4% in primary schools and 26.8% in secondary schools) was well above the national average. The percentage of children with a statement of needs was 1.9%, below the national average of 2.1%. It had a high minority ethnic population (53%) and many pupils had English as a second language. Attainment on entry to school and later was generally high for London. One of the council's key priorities was to keep the council tax as low as possible. Local Authority 4's secondary pupils were the lowest funded and its primary pupils the second lowest funded of any Inner London Borough. There was a strong emphasis on management in the borough and an OFSTED report published in 2000 commended the authority on developing the capacity of its headteachers and senior managers to manage the improvement of their schools through effective guidance in the use of management information.

The borough defined its own education objectives in terms of 'challenging schools to raise standards, whilst promoting their autonomy in an education service that encourages diversity and increases parental choice'. To pursue these management goals, the borough had developed systems to track the progress of individual pupils and was therefore able to judge how different schools were performing in value added terms. Rigorous improvement targets were set for schools in relation to management information systems.

The emphasis on parental choice was evident in the pattern of secondary education, where 34% of parents chose out-of-borough or independent schools. Significant numbers of pupils from less affluent neighbouring boroughs moved into the borough's secondary schools. The borough's eighty schools had diverse systems of governance, and included voluntary aided, community and foundation schools as well as schools with Beacon and specialist college status. Choice and diversity were also key themes in the borough's special educational needs strategy. Following the abolition of the Inner London Education Authority, the borough was left with more than ten special schools. Recently three of these had closed, but a relatively high proportion of children continued to be educated in special schools (57% of all children with statements). The borough had a policy of promoting inclusion and 43% of children with statements attended mainstream schools. There was some concern among the special schools that many of the special schools were running at under-capacity, leading to increased unit costs.

Parents were well informed of their rights and since 1998 had been assisted by the Parent Partnership Service. Parents' Forum meetings were held on a termly basis and annual parents' conferences were well supported by parents and carers. The borough had a relatively high proportion of appeals to the Special Educational Needs Tribunal. In 1999/2000, 16 appeals were heard. Fifty six appeals were registered between 1997 and 2000, although of these 40% were withdrawn before the hearing took place. The

Table 5: Model Features of English Local Authority 4

Models	Features	
BUREAUCRACY	High level of reliance on criteria in decision-making. Many decisions taken by individual officers working alone with no opportunity of colleague offering a second opinion. (Decisions taken either by Panel or individual officers.) Appeared to some interviewees (ie some parents, LASSD care workers, some teachers, officer) as relatively inflexible especially when parental request was for school placement in neighbouring LEA. This would be refused if LEA had available places. School allocation considered to be dependent on too narrow a set of definitions of the SEN categories ascribed to special schools.	NB: Membership of the Panel split almost equally between officers and professionals.
PROFESSION-ALISM	EPs generally perceived to have most influence. Seen as central to whole process. Acknowledged by all groups of interviewees, including officers, that contents of statements drew more on EP advice than other advice. EPs saw themselves as working on behalf of the child. EPs identified by both parents and LASSD care workers as gate-keepers to statutory assessment for pre-school children. Parents received copies of reports before receiving the proposed statement.	NB: EPs held no gate-keeper role for school-age children. EPs said they had no more power or influence than any other report-writer when decision is made who gets a statement. EPs valued working in this way.
LEGALITY	50% take-up of service offered by the PPC meant parents well informed of rights and the SEN procedures. Relatively high level of SENT appeals showed active parent body. Parents received copies of reports before receiving the proposed statement – allows time to make decision on appeal. Active vol orgs support parents bringing cases.	NB: Senior officer believed inevitable tension between LEA's concern with overall provision & Tribunal's concern with individual case. If outcome depends on quality of legal representation, then maverick judgements may be made. V few cases from parents from minority ethnic groups.

MANAGERIA-LISM	Handbook issued to all staff setting out procedures. Performance indicator of time taken to open a Statement of Needs published. Concern to adhere to recommended timescales. Strict criteria used to determine whether to open a Statement and level of resourcing.	NB: Strict timescales mean less time for consultation, visiting schools etc. Pressure from senior officers and elected members on case managers.
CONSUMERISM	Parents received assessment reports prior to draft statement. High level of appeals and complaints to ombudsman. High use of Parent Partnership Service and Named Persons. Termly parents' forum meeting and annual parents' conference. Evidence that middle class parents drove procedures. Active vol orgs including some campaigning for inclusion and some to defend special schools.	NB: Efforts by Parent Partnership Co-ordinator to extend voice to socially disadvantaged parents. Believed this was LEA's strong point c.f. neighbouring authorities
MARKETS	High level of appeals to do with named school. Some over-subscribed selective schools. Mainstream school not obliged to take child if full. Even if place available, LEA reluctant to force headteacher to take child. Particular problem finding placement for children with behavioural difficulties.	NB: LEA reluctant to agree to placement in independent school or outwith authority.

appeals mostly concerned refusal of the local authority to make a statutory assessment or the school named in the statement. In 1999/2000, 70% of cases were won by the local authority. In addition to appeals to the SENT, nine complaints, concerning alleged delay to type of provision, had been made to the Commissioner for Local Administration. The ombudsman had decided either not to investigate or, where there had been an investigation, that no maladministration had been found. Since the LEA had tightened up its procedures, opening virtually all its statements within the prescribed timescale, complaints had become rare.

As summarised in Table 5, Local Authority 4 exemplified many features of new managerialism, characterised by high levels of delegation from the centre to the schools, but with control from the centre maintained by the strict management of performance.

Within the field of SEN, this was exemplified by the insistence on adherence to strict time limits and procedures for statutory assessment and statementing. Two area-based teams of case managers were responsible for the management of assessment and statementing and their role was clearly separated from that of the educational psychologists, whose remit was to offer professional advice on the difficulties and needs of particular children. All systems were computerised and standard letters were issued automatically once the assessment procedure was initiated. The Senior Officer said that the 18 week deadline in issuing the draft statement and the 26 week deadline for issuing the final statement imposed great pressures on case managers, who were closely scrutinised by senior officers and elected members. These pressures were passed on to professionals and parents themselves. Even if parental agreement had not been secured, the local authority often issued the draft statement, in the knowledge that the SENT would automatically find against them if there was any delay. The tight timescale for the production of the final statement sometimes meant that parents did not have enough time to visit all the schools they were considering.

A decision on issuing a statement was made by a panel with reference to tightly specified criteria, which were used to place each child in a band according to the extent of their additional needs. This was to ensure consistency and fairness in resource allocation and each child's banding was regularly reviewed. The Parent Partnership Co-ordinator commented that in her view the local authority's systems were 'fair and they treat everybody the same'. This helped to overcome social class injustices which might otherwise arise. The application of very strict criteria was not only perceived to be fair, but also served the LEA's policy objective of reducing the number of children with Statements of Need. The down-side of this bureaucratic approach was that, although professionals were involved in the decision-making process, their ability to bend rules in unusual cases was reduced, leading parents to perceive the system as inflexible.

It was evident that Local Authority 4 had undergone a significant cultural change since the 1980s, replacing traditional systems of bureaucracy and professionalism with a new modus operandi based on legality, managerialism, consumerism and markets. Whilst the Senior Officer made it clear that local authority officers were pressurised by these systems, she felt that the use of clear criteria in the system meant that outcomes were fair. She also endorsed the strengthening of parents' rights through the SEN Tribunal, because if the authority had followed proper procedures then the SENT was likely to adjudicate in their favour. The presence of an independent body empowered to make a final decision meant that disputes could be finally resolved. In order to avoid appeals, which staff found very stressful, the local authority had made active efforts to engage parents in the process through the Parent Partnership Service. The Parent Partnership Co-ordinator focused in particular on engaging socially disadvantaged parents who might otherwise be alienated from the process. This helped to counteract the negative trade-off of consumerist, rights and market approaches, which tend to empower those who already enjoy considerable social advantage. The Senior Officer felt, however, that a fundamental tension remained between the Tribunal, which was concerned with individual cases, and the LEA, which was concerned with overall provision. The digest of SENT cases included a rider pointing out that similar cases in the future might lead to different outcomes because of their individual nature. By taking a case to the SENT, it might be possible for a child with less significant difficulties to obtain disproportionately expensive provision and this raised difficult equal opportunities concerns. In addition, if the outcome depended on the quality of legal representation, then this was likely to produce less favourable outcomes for those who were unrepresented.

The Senior Officer also noted that that highly marketised character of education in Local Authority 4 had a negative effect on children with SEN, particularly those with behavioural difficulties. Selective schools were heavily over-subscribed and could legitimately refuse a place to a pupil with SEN. Even if a place was available, devolved school management, particularly in relation to admissions and exclusions, meant that the LEA was reluctant to challenge a headteacher's decision not to admit a child. The choices of parents of children with SEN also had a marked effect on the system. Some middle class parents with dyslexic children requested a place in an independent residential school costing £20,000 a year. The local authority often refused such requests because it felt it had adequate provision within the borough. However, such cases were likely to be appealed.

Overall, Local Authority 4 had strong features of legality, managerialism, consumerism and markets and features of these models tended to reinforce each other. Bureaucracy and professionalism were also evident though muted; whilst educational psychologists played an important role in the process, they were not allowed to orchestrate proceedings or make final decisions on placement. Managerialism had replaced post-war bureaucracy, in that procedures were not simply laid out, but were rigorously enforced and there was a major emphasis on improving performance and delivering services shaped by consumer input.

Conclusion

This chapter has illustrated the tensions between different policy frameworks in local authorities in Scotland and England. Whilst there was evidence of all policy frameworks in each local authority, in Scotland professionalism and bureaucracy continued to hold sway, whereas in the English authorities a greater repertoire of policy models was drawn upon. As noted in Chapter 2, each policy framework involved a different set of positive and negative trade-offs. In the two Scottish authorities, the bureaucratic models offered consistency and professionals tried to service the best interests of their clients, although in Local Authority 2 they were sometimes frustrated by their dual role as agent of the local authority and guardian of their clients' best interests. The negative trade-offs in these authorities were that parents had fewer opportunities to act as critical consumers, choosing between different types of provision and influencing the nature of the services on offer. They also lacked an accessible appeal mechanism if insoluble conflict occurred with the local authority.

In both English authorities, the influence of a wider range of policy frameworks was evident, with a growing emphasis on legality, managerialism, consumerism and markets. Here, too, both positive and negative trade-offs were apparent. Whilst the system allowed parents greater choice, not all were able to fulfil the role of critical consumer. In the London borough, there was a perception that middle class parents might be able to exert more influence to get the services they wanted and to appeal if dissatisfied. It was certainly the case that very few parents in the northern authority with high levels of social disadvantage were engaged in choosing services, using Parent Partnership Schemes or appealing if dissatisfied. By the same token, the managerialist regime, characterised by the setting of strict targets, placed professionals under pressure and allowed them less time to work creatively with parents.

Overall, it was clear that, whilst national policies were implemented differently in specific local contexts, there was a tendency in Scotland to draw more exclusively on a narrower range of policy frameworks. As noted in Chapter 2, this may change in the future with the reform of the system of recording, which may give parents greater rights of appeal. The extent to which this will challenge the dominance of professionalism and bureaucracy remains to be seen.

CHAPTER 4

DEFINING AND MEASURING INCLUSION

Introduction
Official policy documents at national and local level all express a commitment to inclusion. However, there is a lack of conceptual clarity about what inclusion means and how it is to be achieved. Clarifying what is meant by inclusion is of growing importance given the passage of the Standards in Scotland's Schools etc (Scotland) Act 2000 and the SEN & Disability Act 2001, both of which imply a greater commitment to inclusive education in the future. In this chapter, we consider the evolution of thinking about integration and inclusion, some of the reasons for conceptual confusion, and ways of measuring inclusion. Finally, we consider some future directions for conceptualising, operationalising and measuring inclusion.

Defining inclusion
As noted in Chapter 1, there has always been some tension between the drive to create more specialist provision for children with SEN and the desire to include as many children as possible in mainstream schools. Drives for inclusive policies have always been influenced by budgetary considerations, since special schools with favourable teacher pupil ratios are very expensive. On the other hand, providing high levels of support to children with SEN in mainstream classes is also expensive, since peripatetic support staff must be paid for. At the same time, social inclusion policies have led to the rejection of segregated forms of provision, whether these take the form of long-stay hospitals or special schools.

The Warnock Report (DES, 1978) provided a very strong endorsement of the principle of integration, referring to it as 'the central contemporary issue in special education'. Warnock argued:

> The principle of educating handicapped and non-handicapped children together, which is described as 'integration' in this country and 'mainstreaming' in the United States of America, and is recognised as a much wider movement of 'normalisation' in Scandinavia and Canada, is the particular expression of a widely held and still growing conviction that, as far as is humanly possible, handicapped people should share the opportunities for self-fulfilment enjoyed by other people. (para 7.1 p 99)

Despite this support for integration, special schools were seen by the Warnock Committee as offering positive educational experiences to some disabled children as a result of favourable resourcing arrangements.

With regard to the principle of choice, Warnock promoted the idea of partnership with parents in pursuit of the child's best interests. The report did not embrace fully the notion of parent as final arbiter of appropriate educational provision and was criticised by commentators such as Kirp (1982) for failing to endorse a rights approach and reinforcing the principle of professional discretion. Overall, Warnock, represented a cautious compromise, supporting partnership with parents but failing to challenge professionals' ultimate control over decision-making. Similarly, whilst endorsing the principle of integration, the ongoing role of special schools was affirmed.

In conceptualising integration, Warnock made a distinction between locational, social and functional integration. Locational integration would be used to describe a situation where children with SEN were educated on the same site as other children, but tended to receive most of their education in a special unit. Social integration would be used to describe a higher level of contact between the disabled child and others, so that all children would spend recreation and lunch periods together, but would otherwise be educated separately for much of the time. The term functional integration would be used to refer to a situation where disabled children were spending their entire school day in a mainstream setting. Whilst receiving additional support, they would be following essentially the same curriculum as other children in the class. Warnock's distinction has come to be regarded as too fixed and static. However, distinguishing between different types of integration is useful because it reminds us that, whilst the broad educational goals may be the same for all children, the precise targets and means of achieving these will be different. For example, it would be unreasonable to expect a child with complex difficulties to be taking three Highers. Whilst this may appear to be a rather obvious statement, some writing in this area seems to imply that all children should have precisely the same learning goals at all times.

As noted in Chapter 1, a rather different balance was struck by a report from Scottish HMI (SED, 1978) which argued for a much stronger commitment to the integration of children with learning difficulties into mainstream classes. Indeed, in the view of HMI, withdrawing children into segregated remedial classes tended to accentuate rather than alleviate their difficulties and distract attention from the central source of problems, the curriculum in mainstream schools. In this document, the principle of integration was seen as more important than the individual parent's right to choose their child's educational placement.

Yet another variation on the balance between the principles of integration and choice was struck by the 1980 Education (Scotland) Act (as amended). This legislation made no mention of educating children with special educational needs in mainstream classes, although provision for parental choice of school was extended to parents of children with special educational needs. It was assumed that parents who wished to do so would choose to have their children educated in a mainstream school. A range of caveats restricted the extent to which parents were able to exercise choices. If unreasonable additional expense were to be incurred by placing a child in a mainstream school, or the placement might be detrimental to the education of other children, then a parent's request for a mainstream placement could be refused. Integration was not seen as an essential component of the system, but as an option to be taken up if it accorded with parental wishes and if the authority was able to resource it. If provision were to move in this direction, then parental choice had to be the engine of change in accordance with market principles. At this stage, the child's preferences were not seen as a major deciding factor.

Subsequently, the discourse of integration was replaced by the discourse of inclusion. Corbett and Slee (2000), for example, drew a distinction between integration and inclusion. Integration was described as 'inherently assimilationist', forcing learners to fit into a uni-cultural 'mono-dimensional' mainstream. Inclusion, on the other hand, was seen as essentially transformative, fundamentally challenging 'existing hierarchies of status and privilege'. Armstrong et al (2000) described integration and inclusion as 'two opposing political goals'. Noting the establishment of this dichotomy between integration and inclusion, Booth (2000) suggested that attempts to see integration as synonymous with assimilation and inclusion as synonymous with transformation was an example of formulaic thinking which served to confuse, rather than clarify, the issue.

In support of this contention, Booth noted that early writing on integration, including the rather mild suggestions of the Warnock Committee, were regarded as extremely radical and threatening by the special education establishment who feared an attack on special schools. Sally Tomlinson's work on the sociology of special education (Tomlinson, 1982) similarly attracted considerable attacks from academics located within the educational psychology tradition, who considered that critical analysis of the grounds on which children were selected for 'special educational treatment' implied a rejection of the need for any additional support.

Booth also noted that, whilst some writing in the 'integration' tradition had quite radical implications, some work which espoused principles of inclusion was actually quite unthreatening. For example, the Tomlinson report on *Inclusive Learning* (Tomlinson, 1997) defined inclusion as 'matching the resources we have to the learning styles and educational needs of the students'. In fairness, it should be noted that the report was about further education, where the diversity of the student population and the vocational mission of the sector make inclusion very difficult. Nonetheless, this definition is extremely minimalist, saying nothing about where young people with SEN should be educated and the extent to which high-level educational goals should be common to all. The idea of 'needs' is treated as unproblematic, although it appears that these will be defined by educators and reflect what is deliverable without the need for major change.

Finally, Booth drew attention to the fact that, whilst the UK Government places a great deal of emphasis on its social inclusion agenda, this often fails to connect with the education of children with SEN. In Scotland, greater efforts have been made to link school inclusion with the wider social inclusion agenda. For example, the document *Special Educational Needs in Scotland* (Scottish Office, 1998) stated:

> An inclusive society must ensure that the potential of each individual is fully developed through education and that their attainment and achievement are valued and respected. It is on the realisation of this potential that inclusiveness depends; an inclusive society and education system will therefore strive to ensure that it creates the range of approaches and opportunities to ensure that this is brought about.

Similar views were expressed in the Scottish Parliament's Report on the Inquiry into Special Educational Needs (Scottish Parliament Education, Culture and Sport Committee, 2001). Despite the widespread endorsement of inclusion, most official documents acknowledge the need for some form of segregated provision. Whilst the Learning Disabilities Review *The Same as You?* (Scottish Executive, 2000a) stated that fewer children with learning disabilities should be educated in segregated settings, the Government's 29 social justice milestones do not include targets to do with the inclusion of disabled children (Scottish Executive, 2000b).

To summarise, inclusion may appear, on the face of it, to be a more radical concept than integration, but there is no agreement about an operational definition. As a result, it is possible for a wide range of practices to be described as inclusive and the absence of clearly defined goals means that there is no way of measuring whether the inclusion of children with SEN is actually happening. In addition, until relatively recently there has been very little published research on how to improve the learning and teaching of children with special educational needs in mainstream settings. An exception to this is the edited collection of papers produced by Wearmouth (2001), which provides important insights into the effectiveness of particular classroom strategies. For example, Mercer (2001) described the classroom conditions which facilitate the effective learning of children with special needs and others. Children were explicitly taught the rules for effective small group interaction and were then encouraged to implement them to carry out carefully structured tasks. A paper (Merrett, 2000) described the application of peer tutoring techniques in the teaching of reading. Finally, Pickles (2000) described the incorporation of therapy into the mainstream curriculum for children with severe motor difficulties. Such studies acknowledge that children with particular impairments need additional assistance to remove learning barriers. The development of an evidence base of what works in the everyday practice of inclusion is essential to the successful implementation of inclusive policies in the classroom. Appeals to teachers to treat all children equally are unlikely to have much effect on changing received practices.

Why are inclusive policies so difficult in practice?
A somewhat paradoxical situation exists, therefore, in which there is strong official endorsement of educational inclusion, but very little shared knowledge about how this is to be achieved and how success may be assessed. In the following sections, some possible explanations of the difficulties encountered in implementing inclusive policies are explored.

(i) Tensions between inclusion and choice
As has been noted, the official endorsement of school inclusion has grown, but at the same time it has been acknowledged that various forms of specialist provision will continue to exist and certainly no targets have been suggested for the closure of special schools. One reason for this is that parental choice continues to be a major element in educational policy. *The Parents' Charter for Scotland* (Scottish Office, 1991) initially set out the principles of consumerism which were to inform the fourth term of the Conservative administration. These included the following principles which were to apply in all public sector services:

- a sustained new programme for improving quality;
- an emphasis on choice, wherever possible between competing providers, as the best spur to quality improvement;
- the citizen's right to be told what service standards are and to be assured of action when service is unacceptable; and
- the need for public services to give value for money within a tax bill the nation can afford.

Involving parents more fully in decision-making about their children's education has continued to be an important theme in Scottish education policy.

This emphasis on choice and accountability to parents has particular implications for special needs education, because it is evident that parents tend to have very different views of whether mainstream or special education is preferable. Many parents of disabled children are involved in their child's special school through activities such as fund-raising and there is sometimes a strong attachment between special schools and their local communities which means that proposals to close special schools are likely to provoke a strong adverse reaction. Over recent years, as 'new disabilities' such as Attention Deficit Hyperactive Disorder have been identified, growing numbers of parents have argued the case for education in special schools or units where they expect to find staff trained in specific instructional techniques rather than in generic learning support approaches. On the other hand, there are groups such Equity, with a large parent membership, who campaign for inclusive education. They acknowledge that parents should continue to have choice, but believe that the reason many parents opt for special schooling is because of an absence of resources in mainstream. When parents have such polarised views, the development of a consensus on policy goals is obviously very difficult.

(ii) Tensions between individual and group provision
As noted above, parents of children with SEN may be sceptical about the benefits of inclusive education because of doubts with regard to the capacity and commitment of mainstream schools to meet their child's special educational needs. The development of special needs education has generally been informed by the idea that a very small group of children have disabilities which makes it difficult or impossible for them to be educated alongside their peers without additional resources. Special schools, as noted in Chapter 1, have traditionally had much better teacher pupil ratios and specialist equipment. The process of assessment and recording was intended to identify which children had special needs, the nature of these additional needs and the additional resources that would be required. It was expected that the additional resources specified would be funded by the local authority, rather than being paid for from the school's budget. According to some evidence presented to the Scottish Executive as part of its consultation on assessment and recording, this produced perverse incentives, leading schools to encourage parents to seek assessments so that additional resources would flow into the school.

   Evidence given to the Scottish Executive from the Association of Scottish Principal Educational Psychologists as part of this consultation suggested an alternative way of resourcing special educational needs, described as an entitlement model. According to such a model, an annual audit takes place of the level of need in particular schools. Information from the audit is used to inform a funding model, and all resources are devolved to school level. The responsibility then rests with the particular school to meet the educational needs of all children within that school. Rather than allocating a certain number of hours to individual children, funds would be used to provide high levels of background learning support, so that learning difficulties can be prevented from arising in the first place and children who are having difficulties may be helped without delay. This model of resourcing places a great deal of responsibility on the professionalism of educational psychologists and teachers to assess needs accurately and ensure that resources are fairly distributed. Evidence to the Scottish Executive consultation given by some parents of children with SEN, however, indicated some scepticism with regard to the effectiveness of an entitlement model in meeting the needs of particular children with SEN. Some parents felt that unless resources were targeted at an individual child, they might receive very little one-to-one support and, as a result, fail to thrive in mainstream.

It would of course be quite possible to have inclusive policies which allowed resources to be targeted on individual children. However, because inclusion is often associated with a rejection of individually targeted funding, some parents have become suspicious that inclusion may in reality lead to a reduction in the amount of money spent on disabled children.

(iii) Tensions between curriculum entitlement and the developmental curriculum

When the 5–14 Curriculum in Scotland and the National Curriculum in England were developed, there was considerable ambivalence about their relevance to pupils with SEN. It was argued by some that for children with severe and profound learning difficulties, who would be largely focusing on developmental matters, there was little point in participating in a common curriculum and assessment framework. Others, such as Heward and Lloyd-Smith (1990) and Hegarty (1989) argued that for children with SEN there was much to be gained from being included in a national curriculum and assessment framework. Practitioners, it was suggested, would be forced to think much more carefully about teaching and assessment methods. In addition, parents had a right to accessible information about educational targets and progress. In England, a formal system was put in place for the 'disapplication' of the national curriculum and assessment. A case had to be made in relation to each child who was to be given exemption. In Scotland, where approaches to the curriculum and assessment were less prescriptive, the Scottish Office Education Department sated that testing should 'be left to the discretion of the school in consultation with the parent of the pupil' (SOED, 1991: para 16.3).

It was expected that, in England, many applications for the exemption would be made, but in reality these were relatively rare. Some time after the publication of the main curriculum documents, advice was published in both Scotland and England on how to adapt the curriculum and assessment for children with SEN. In addition, children with SEN have been included in more recent target-setting initiatives. Nonetheless, among teachers of children with SEN and their parents there continues to be some ambivalence about whether this group should be treated as essentially the same as other children, or essentially different. Recognising difference for this group, as for many others, brings both advantages and disadvantages. For children with SEN, being identified as different may bring some apparent advantages, such as more individual attention and smaller classes. On the other hand, it may also bring stigma and have a damaging impact on post-school opportunities. Differences between parents and professionals in relation to inclusion often hinge on differing perceptions of the relative advantages and disadvantages of this 'special' identity, played out in differing views of the extent to which children with SEN should be expected automatically to participate in the mainstream curriculum and assessment.

(iv) Tensions within the disability movement

The disability movement is a growing political force within the UK and has argued powerfully for the abolition of separate provision for children with special educational needs. Segregated provision has been identified as one of the major factors reinforcing the inferiority of disabled children (see, for example, the accounts of Barnes, 1991 and Mason, 1993). Similar moves towards entirely inclusive systems of education are also evident in other parts of the industrialised world. For example, in Canada the existence of special classes has been challenged under provincial Human Rights Codes and the Canadian Charter of Rights and Freedoms. Inclusion has been seen as a 'pressing human rights issue', and the segregation of disabled children in special schools has been compared with the historical segregation of black people.

The disability movement would have little truck with the argument that some parents might wish to choose education in special settings. Such choices, it would be argued, simply reflect the fact that insufficient resources have been allocated to mainstream schools and the answer is to increase funding in mainstream and remove the additional resourcing given to special schools which makes them, for some parents, more attractive options. The issue becomes more complicated, however, because some disabled people themselves argue for separate specialist provision. Corker (1998), for example, describes the historical tensions between Deaf culture and the disability movement, as deaf people struggle to achieve cultural autonomy based on the use of sign language. People who identify with Deaf culture see themselves not as disabled, but as a linguistic minority requiring sign-language medium education just as some Gaelic-speakers argue for Gaelic medium education. Other groups, such as blind people, may defend the principle of separate school systems where Braille may be taught to academically able blind children. The fact that the disability movement has discovered deep internal divisions in relation to inclusive education has made it difficult to hold a simple and consistent position.

To summarise, integration and inclusion have sometimes been presented as diametrically opposed concepts and inclusion has tended to be defined rhetorically rather than operationally. Until relatively recently, there has been little research on effective teaching and learning in inclusive settings. Whilst official policy documents tend to endorse inclusion, inclusive practices have developed rather slowly because of a commitment to the principle of parental choice of school, uncertainty about resource models, the idea of an entitlement curriculum and divisions within the disability movement. Progress has also been stymied by a lack of reliable data on the extent to which moves towards inclusion are taking place. The following section summarises lessons to be learnt from official statistics.

Are we moving towards more inclusive policies?

The Scottish Executive conducts an annual schools census which collects data on all pupils in schools. The number and location of pupils with records of needs in particular authorities was recorded, as well as their principal learning difficulty. These data should provide information on progress toward inclusion over time. However, the data are difficult to interpret, partly because there are no firm criteria for opening a record of needs, which has led to variation in local practice. In 1999, education authorities were required to provide data on children with special educational needs as well as those with records of needs. The Scottish Executive did not specify any criteria for defining a child as having special educational needs, and this category was interpreted even more widely than the record of needs category.

Table 6 illustrates variability between authorities in the proportion of children for whom a record of needs is opened and who are identified as having special educational needs. With regard to the record of needs, whilst the Scottish average is about 2% the range is from 0.8% in East Dunbartonshire to almost 3% in Inverclyde. The Scottish average for pupils with SEN is slightly less than 5%. The range within this category is from 1.8% in East Dunbartonshire to almost 8% in Stirling. The extent to which children with SEN have records of needs is also variable. In South Lanarkshire, 59% of children with SEN have records of needs. In West Lothian, records of needs are only opened for 26% of such children.

One measure of inclusion is the extent to which children with records of needs are being educated in mainstream or special settings. Figure 1 shows the percentage of children in mainstream and special schools by educating authority. This shows that Angus, East Lothian, Moray and Scottish Borders educated all recorded children in mainstream schools. Education authorities with low rates of mainstreaming were Glasgow (19%), West Dunbartonshire (33%) and Edinburgh (35%). However, these figures are misleading for a number of reasons:

- 27% of children in special settings did not have a record of needs. (However, such children were covered by the 1980 Act and therefore had a legal entitlement to a record. Rights to appeal, to have a regular review and a multi-disciplinary assessment are removed in the absence of a record of needs).
- Some children placed in special units had their name on the register of a mainstream school. They might, however, spend most of their time in a segregated setting.
- Figures refer to educating, not funding, authority. Edinburgh and Glasgow imported children from surrounding areas because of their historical legacy of special schools. As a result, it appeared that some authorities made virtually no use of special placements, whilst others make very high use. Both sets of figures are misleading.

A further measure of the extent of inclusion is the proportion of the school population in special schools (see Figure 1). Across Scotland, 1.2% of the school population was educated in a special school or unit in 1999. This

Table 6: Number and percentage of pupils with records of needs and special educational needs in Scottish education authorities

	No. of pupils with RoN	% of all pupils	No. of pupils with SEN	% of all pupils	% of SEN pupils with RoN
Scotland	15,643	1.9	37,702	4.8	41.5
Aberdeen City	793	2.6	1,656	5.6	44.1
Aberdeenshire	646	1.7	2,064	5.6	32.9
Angus	277	1.7	630	3.8	42.9
Argyll & Bute	159	1.1	730	5.3	24.7
Clackmannanshire	182	2.1	570	6.6	31.8
Dumfries & Galloway	484	2.1	1,653	7.4	28.3
Dundee City	585	2.6	957	4.4	58.5
East Ayrshire	423	2.2	905	4.7	48.7
East Dunbartonshire	151	0.8	360	1.8	47.2
East Lothian	121	0.9	270	2.0	40.4
East Renfrewshire	217	1.4	864	5.4	24.7
Edinburgh	1,057	1.7	3,582	5.9	29.9
Eilean Siar	108	2.4	285	6.7	40.7
Falkirk	531	2.5	1,122	5.3	54.0
Fife	583	1.1	2,244	4.2	28.6
Glasgow City	2,355	2.7	3,842	4.5	61.9
Highland	869	2.6	2,086	6.2	40.1
Inverclyde	393	2.8	775	5.6	54.1
Midlothian	186	1.4	436	3.3	39.0
Moray	294	2.0	822	5.7	40.0
North Ayrshire	486	2.2	968	4.4	48.0
North Lanarkshire	905	1.7	1,809	3.4	51.2
Orkney Islands	43	1.3	171	5.4	25.1
Perth & Kinross	383	1.8	875	4.2	44.0
Renfrewshire	813	2.9	1,931	7.0	46.2
Scottish Borders	255	1.6	882	5.7	30.0
Shetland Islands	78	2.0	190	4.9	43.2
South Ayrshire	364	2.0	834	4.8	47.0
South Lanarkshire	960	2.0	1,725	3.5	58.7
Stirling	232	1.8	1,013	7.7	20.5
West Dunbartonshire	139	0.9	422	2.7	32.0
West Lothian	255	1.0	1,040	4.1	26.3

Source: September 1999 School Census

Figure 1: *Pupils with records of needs in mainstream and special schools (%) in Scottish education authorities by educating authority, Schools Cencus 1999*

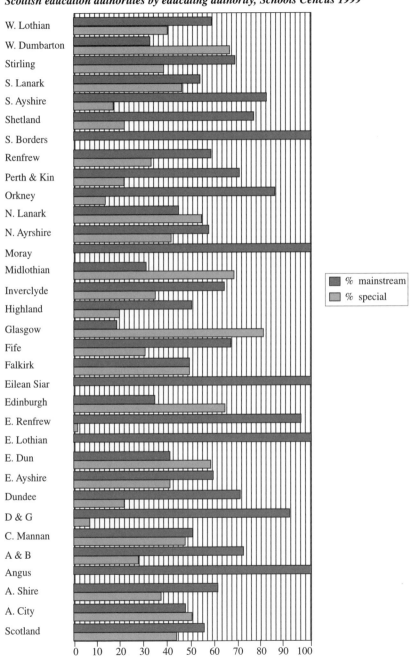

had changed little over the past decade, although there had been a slight increase over recent years. Authorities making high use of special schools were Glasgow (2.6%), Edinburgh (1.5%) and Aberdeen (1.6%). Authorities making little use of special schools were Angus (0.3%), Dumfries and Galloway (0.3%), Fife (0.4%) and Borders (0.4%). Caution is again needed in interpreting these figures because a child whose name is on a mainstream roll may in reality spend little time in a special unit attached to mainstream class. The general trend in Scotland is towards an increased use of special units and a decreased use of special schools. To illustrate this point, in 1995, there were 201 special schools and 143 special units. In 1998 there were 228 special schools and 256 special units.

To summarise, because the criteria for having a record of needs or SEN have never been clearly defined, the statistics are difficult to interpret and provide little firm evidence of a move towards inclusion. This is further complicated by uncertainty over what counts as a mainstream placement. Some rural areas like Scottish Borders and Dumfries and Galloway had either no or very few special schools. In these areas, children with SEN were often placed in special units attached to mainstream and counted as being in mainstream. However, there might be considerable variation in the amount of time spent with mainstream peers.

Conclusion
Inclusive education policies are evidently an area where greater clarity of thought would be helpful. If the many expressions of commitment to inclusive education for children with SEN are to become a reality, there is a need for a clearer definition of inclusion which might recognise that the goals of inclusion are likely to be different for individual children. The Scottish Executive is, at the time of writing, developing a National Inclusion Strategy, and this should be helpful in providing new directions for policy development. It is important that more attention is paid to identifying targets for inclusion and monitoring progress towards these targets. To do this adequately, what counts as a mainstream placement must be clearly defined. If the Scottish Executive's proposals for Co-ordinated Support Plans are implemented, there will be a need to monitor annually the number of children who have such plans and the nature of their difficulties. For the new policy to be implemented consistently, it will be necessary for the Scottish Executive to issue clear guidance on which children should have such plans. Similarly, it will be important to publish clear criteria in relation to the staged processes of assessment and gather data by local authority on the number of children at each level and the nature of their impairments. Research is needed on how inclusion may be practised successfully in different educational settings and for different groups of children. Such work will serve to dissipate rhetoric and increase clarity of thinking about what are reasonable and attainable goals. Finally, the publication *For Scotland's Children* (Scottish Executive, 2001) sets out some of the principles and

challenges involved in the delivery of integrated children's services. There is clearly a need for the sharing of data between education, health and social work to assist in monitoring service delivery and children's progress. This information could also be used to track and compare the relative success of different authorities in creating more inclusive systems.

CHAPTER 5

SOCIAL INCLUSION AND RAISING STANDARDS: COMPETING AGENDAS IN THE FIELD OF SPECIAL EDUCATIONAL NEEDS

Introduction
For at least a decade and a half, there has been a growing concern to ensure the accountability of public services including education. Whereas the New Right's focus on accountability was fuelled by a belief that the public sector was prone to inefficiency, Scottish and UK New Labour administrations have attempted to link the raising standards agenda with the school inclusion and social justice agendas. This chapter explores the nature of accountability policies in relation to special educational needs and presents findings from a Scottish Executive funded research project on a national initiative which attempted to monitor the attainment of targets set within Individualised Educational Programmes (IEPs) by children with SEN (Banks et al, 2001).

Accountability and Audit in the Public Sector
By the 1980s, there was a growing consensus that public sector services were in need of reform. Dissatisfaction with the quality and responsiveness of public services was driven in part by the growing demands of service users for more individually-tailored rather than standardised services. These dissatisfactions were exploited by the New Right, which suggested that much tighter management was needed to ensure value for money, efficiency and effectiveness. A new managerialist approach was advocated, informed by the ideas of US liberal economists such as von Hayek, who argued that the welfare state should be no more than a safety net for those in greatest need. According to Pollitt (1993), the central thesis of the new public management was that everything to do with the human activities of work could and should be measured, and that this was the basis of effective management. Tight audit procedures were required to ensure the delivery of value for money and to guard against the self-serving tendencies of public sector professionals and workers.

Prime Minister James Callaghan, in his Ruskin College speech of 1976, signalled his government's dissatisfaction with school performance and, had the Labour Party been elected in 1979, it would almost certainly have sought to increase public sector accountability through the audit of school and local authority performance. Instead, the election of a Conservative

Government in that year led to the adoption of a new right version of public sector management closely wedded to the wider policy goal of public sector marketisation. From the start of the Conservative administration's third term of office in 1987, the reform of education moved to centre stage and the application of private sector management principles was identified as the central means of infusing education with a competitive, market-orientated ethos (Deakin, 1994). As reflected in the recent White Paper *Modernising Government* (Cabinet Office, 1999), the Westminster and Holyrood administrations have promoted the audit culture (Power, 1997) establishing Best Value as the governing regime of all public services and promoting a mixed economy of service delivery by the public, private and voluntary sectors.

Despite the policy continuities of the Conservative and New Labour governments, the underpinning discourse of public accountability has shifted, with New Labour distancing itself from the Conservative's neo-liberal objectives and attempting to use audit technologies as a means of modernising the welfare state (Fergusson, 2000). The overall impact of the growing centrality of audit and accountability continues to be debated. Some commentators have suggested that accountability regimes may have different purposes, methods and serve a range of political goals. For example, Fairley and Paterson (1995) distinguished between market, bureaucratic and democratic versions of accountability. Others, for instance Power (1997), suggested that the expansion of accountability and audit may be indicative of a breakdown of social trust and the effects of audit must be carefully monitored because of the tendency to produce a range of dysfunctional responses within organisations. One such response was described by Power as colonisation, and occurs when the goals of the organisation become taken over by the performance indicators which are assessed. As a result, the organisation loses sight of its own objectives and values.

An alternative response was described in terms of decoupling. When this takes place, an individual within the organisation takes on responsibility for audit compliance, whilst others continue to pursue their independent goals. Whereas Power accepted that evaluation, assessment, checking and account-giving are part of everyday human interaction, he maintained that an uncritical belief in the efficacy of accountability regimes may produce 'deluded visions of control and transparency which are neither as effective nor as neutral as commonly imagined' (Power, 1997: 143). As noted above, this chapter uses the case of special educational needs to explore the extent to which the dual goals of raising standards and social inclusion are compatible and capable of being achieved through the application of managerialist accountability principles. Before considering the Raising Standards in Special Educational Needs Initiative more closely, it is necessary to consider the history of accountability within Scottish education and the special educational needs system.

Scottish education and accountability

During the 1980s, accountability policies in Scotland, as in England, were driven by the increasingly radical agenda of the Conservative government, although this agenda tended to be implemented in more muted form north of the border. The Parents' Charter in Scotland, first published in 1991 and updated in 1995, emphasised the importance of quality, standards, information, choice and value for money. Within the market model of accountability implicit in the Parents' Charter, service consumers, envisaged as parents rather than children, were seen as the drivers of reform, using readily accessible information to inform rational choices. The (theoretical) outcome of competition between service providers was greater efficiency, effectiveness and value for money, since, in a social re-enactment of Darwinist principles, services which were poorly adapted to market conditions would wither and die, whilst the better adapted would survive and flourish.

Access to simple information was central to the market-driven version of public accountability reflected in the Parents' Charter. The Conservative Government sought ways of providing such information, but the implementation of auditable systems was impeded by the Government's tenuous political legitimacy, which meant that educational reform, whilst drawing from a common UK policy repertoire (McPherson and Raab, 1988), was implemented at a much slower pace. For example, the 5–14 programme (SOED, 1987) was introduced by regulation rather than law, unlike its English counterpart. There was strong resistance to national testing from both teachers and parents, on the grounds that formal assessment was likely to label some children as failures at a very early age and might undermine the principles of comprehensive schooling by creating a hierarchy of schools. As a result of a parental boycott, it was agreed that teachers should base their assessment of pupils on normal teaching activities, using items selected from a national assessment bank, and tests should be administered to individuals or groups of children merely to confirm teachers' judgements that a certain standard had been achieved. Education authorities would not gather or publish information on the tests, thus making league tables of primary schools impossible to compile. It should be noted, however, that standardised tests have subsequently been introduced by education authorities to provide accurate baseline assessment information, justified, in part, as a means of measuring the success of early intervention strategies.

Whilst there was reluctance to publish primary league tables in Scotland, regulations (SOED, 1992a) required schools to publish data on examination results, attendance, school leaver destinations, school costs and policy on special educational needs. Financial devolution to the school level (SOED, 1992b) was justified on the grounds that it empowered school managers to target resources on centrally identified performance indicators. A further boost to the accountability project was the establishment of an Audit Unit within the inspectorate with the task of collecting, analysing and publishing evidence about the performance of schools and education departments. In addition to the publication of documents on standards and quality in Scottish schools based on inspections and performance indicators, the Audit Unit encouraged schools to engage in self-evaluation (SOEID, 1996b), suggesting that performance indicators identified by the school should be used to identify and monitor the achievement of specific, achievable and measurable targets. The implications of giving schools responsibility for their own improvement has been much debated (see, for example, the collection of papers edited by Riddell and Brown, 1991). Whereas commentators like Hargreaves (1990) concluded that schools cannot honestly evaluate themselves due to internal resistance to critical scrutiny, Stoll (1991) argued that school improvement is more likely to be achieved through professionals taking responsibility for their own work, rather than through the external imposition of centralised control.

The emphasis on schools taking responsibility for their own development, with a relatively 'light touch' being exerted by central and local government, accorded well with Scottish resistance to the marketisation of services and general suspicion of the motives of Westminster government. Despite this endorsement of school self-evaluation as the central mechanism of school improvement, the Audit Unit issued warnings about the relatively poor performance of Scottish schools in international league tables and in 1996 the Conservative administration, as one of its last acts, established a Task Force on underachievement in Scottish schools (SOED, 1996c).

The Task Force report was significant in arguing that a tighter audit regime was required to tackle educational inequality rather than to promote a market-driven agenda. It noted problems with basic literacy in disadvantaged areas and recommended that there should be a significant shift from internal school regulation to external accountability. Children's attainments in relation to the 5–14 programme should be reported to education authorities and placed in the public domain, a decisive shift from the earlier position where the school reported the individual child's results to parents. The Task Force endorsed the public reporting of external examination results, but favoured the use of value added data over crude league tables, a decisive shift from HMI's earlier position that taking account of pupil background was simply 'making excuses' for under-achievement. (See Riddell (1997) for discussion of the representation of social class in school effectiveness research). Finally, the Task Force report commended the setting of targets as advocated by the Advisory Scottish Council for Education and Training Targets (ASCETT), drawing on human capital arguments:

> All industrialised nations are in the course of raising educational attainment across their populations. There is a widespread recognition that the quality of education is a major determinant of successful economic competitiveness. (SOEID, 1996c: 5)

The advent of a New Labour government at Westminster and a Labour-Liberal coalition government within the Scottish Parliament at Holyrood provided the conditions for new policy initiatives to emerge after the stalemate of the last years of the Conservative government. Given this opportunity for new beginnings, it is interesting that target-setting should emerge as new Labour's flagship policy (see, for example, the advisory document *Setting Targets — Raising Standards in Schools* (SOEID, 1998b) and the White Paper *Targeting Excellence: Modernising Scotland's Schools* (SOEID, 1999a). There was a strong degree of continuity between Conservative and New Labour education policies in terms of espousing new managerialist policies and practices. However, the justification of these policies was different; whilst both administrations emphasised value for money, the Conservatives promoted consumer choice whilst, for New Labour, social inclusion was the dominant discourse.

The Standards in Scotland's Schools etc. (Scotland) Act 2000 provided the legislative backing for the rigorous, quantifiable and public forms of accountability signalled in the earlier policy papers. Scottish Ministers and Education Authorities were given the responsibility to 'secure improvement in the quality of school education' and a direct duty was placed on Government to identify performance indicators for Scottish education and provide independent, external evaluation of the education functions of local authorities (Scottish Executive, 1999: 15). Education Authorities were given a duty to prepare a statement of improvement objectives in the areas of national priority identified by Scottish Ministers and put in place arrangements to ensure they identify and take action to continuously improve performance in schools (Scottish Executive, 1999: 16). It is now established practice for local authorities to set targets for each school to achieve annually, and, for children with SEN, performance in relation to targets specifies on the IEP is a central part of this assessment.

To summarise, the Scottish Office, and subsequently the Scottish Executive, consistently promoted a managerialist agenda informed by a market-driven version of accountability. However, the Conservative Government's lack of political legitimacy in Scotland meant that a centrally-controlled audit culture was slower to take hold and ran alongside a system based on professional self-regulation. New Labour, having greater political credibility in Scotland partly as a result of its constitutional reforms, intensified educational audit regimes, whilst favouring bureaucratic rather than market-based versions of accountability with social inclusion as the legitimating discourse. Whilst the Scottish Parliament declared its opposition to the publication of primary league tables, since 1999 local newspapers have published primary school league tables based on the proportion of children achieving various levels within the 5–14 programme.

Special educational needs policy in Scotland and accountability
As argued in earlier chapters of this book, educational accountability has been looser in Scotland than in England, particularly in relation to children

with special educational needs. Revised arrangements for national testing, published in 1992, stated that pupils with SEN and those for whom English was not their first language should only be assessed when they had reached level A. These children, it was argued, could not be assessed using existing instruments and the preparation of specialised tests would be too time-consuming and expensive. Responsibility for the education of children with SEN, it was argued, should continue to reside with the professionals, who would determine what to teach and whether pupils were making progress.

Whilst some special education needs professionals welcomed the freedom from the 5–14 programme, other interest groups, including members of the disability movement, pointed out that teachers of disabled children were less accountable than others. In 1993, HMI issued advice on the adaptation of the 5–14 programme for children with special educational needs (SOED, 1993), recommending broad approaches to the curriculum rather than attempting to benchmark knowledge and skills. The publication *Effective Provision for Special Educational Needs* (EPSEN) (SOED, 1994) attempted to specify management principles to ensure quality and standards. Special schools and units were advised to produce development plans and report progress in achieving identified goals on a three-year cycle. Whilst imposing some degree of external accountability, the onus lay with the school to identify institutional targets, establish success criteria and evaluate progress. A higher degree of external accountability was signalled in the growing emphasis on Individualised Educational Programmes, which were variously described as a means of charting the individual child's progress, identifying the educational provision to be made by the school in conjunction with the record of needs, or evaluating the school's effectiveness in relation to aggregating targets achieved by individual children. The first two functions of the IEP were not new, since gearing teaching towards children's individual needs has a long history within special needs education. However, the idea that teachers and schools might be held accountable for the achievement of learning goals was very radical.

Having established the general principle of accountability, subsequent advice (e.g. *Raising Standards — Setting Targets: Targets for Pupils with Special Educational Needs* (SOEID, 1999b), specified audit mechanisms in more detail. After a pilot year in academic session 1999–2000, special schools and units, as well as mainstream schools educating pupils with special educational needs, were required to report to the Scottish Executive all learning goals set for children with special educational needs and the proportion of targets achieved. Schools were advised that IEPs should be opened for all children in special schools and units and all children with records of needs in mainstream schools. In addition, all children in mainstream schools without a record of needs but requiring 'significant planned intervention' should have an IEP. Targets should be set in one or more of the following curriculum areas: communication and language; numeracy; personal and social development. The number of long-term targets to be achieved during the course of a school sessions could range from 1–2 targets within one area of the curriculum to 8–12 or more targets across three areas of the curriculum. The long-term targets for each pupil were to be broken down into about four short-term targets, each of which should be covered in 6–8 weeks. The targets were to be SMART (specific, measurable, achievable, relevant and timely). They might be based on qualitative or quantitative data, and success criteria and evidence should be stipulated at the outset. Deciding whether a target had been achieved would depend, to a greater or lesser extent, on professional judgement. At the end of each school session, the achievement of long-term targets should be recorded and new targets set. At the end of the academic year, aggregated data were to be reported to the Scottish Executive. In schools with a significant number of pupils with SEN, 80% of pupils were expected to achieve 80% of targets. In schools with a small number of pupils with SEN, each pupil was expected to achieve 80% of his or her individual targets. The advice to schools acknowledged that:

> Some pupils with very complex needs and health-related difficulties may show very small incremental changes in a year and may well become less responsive. (SOEID, 1999b, 40: 7)

Nonetheless, all pupils, no matter how significant their needs, were to be included in the target-setting programme. As well as having their IEP target outcomes reported to the Scottish Executive, pupils with SEN were also to be included in the mainstream target-setting exercise. According to the Scottish executive, unless children with SEN were included in the mainstream accountability initiative, this would be seen as anti-inclusive. Some headteachers expressed concerns that that this might militate against the inclusion of disabled children in mainstream schools, but this argument was not accepted by the Scottish Executive, who said that mainstream targets could be adjusted to reflect the proportion of children with SEN.

The target-setting initiative was phased in, with only schools which considered they were ready being fully involved in the first phase, from April 1999 to the end of session 1999/2000. More schools joined in August 1999. From April 2000, all schools were expected to collate information derived from pupils reviews and individual planning meetings in order to develop statements of long-term targets with appropriate success criteria. By August 2000, all schools were expected to have set targets and have systems in place to track progress.

The research project
The project *Raising Standards for Pupils with Special Educational Needs,* commissioned by the Scottish Executive Education Department, ran from January 2000–February 2001. It was undertaken jointly by researchers from the Strathclyde Centre for Disability Research and the St Andrew's Faculty of Education at the University of Glasgow and the Special Educational

Needs Research Centre at the University of Newcastle. The aims of the research were:

• to identify examples of the effective use of IEPs in special schools and units;
• to compare this with the use of IEPs with a small sample of children with special educational needs in mainstream education;
• to explore the relationship between IEPs and raising attainment; and
• to make recommendations for the effective use of IEPs.

The methods used consisted of a literature review, key informant interviews, a questionnaire survey of all special schools and units and a sample of mainstream primary and secondary schools, and case studies of the use of IEPs with children with a range of learning difficulties in mainstream and special settings at primary and secondary levels. Full details of the research are reported in Banks et al (2001). As indicated above, the main concern of this chapter is to explore the implications of strengthening accountability in relation to children with SEN and the compatibility of the raising standards and school inclusion agendas. Some key themes relating to these issues are summarised below.

The history and development of IEPs
Individualised Educational Programmes for children with SEN have developed in many parts of the industrialised world since the 1970s and reflect a range of influences and underlying philosophies of learning. In the 1970s and 1980s, behavioural psychologists occupied a powerful position within the field of special needs education (e.g. Brennan, 1974; Ainscow and Tweddle, 1979). They maintained that if a complex task could be analysed and broken into constituent parts, then each part could be taught until the child was able to undertake the entire activity. The component parts of each task were to be recorded within an IEP. This would be used by the teacher or instructor to record pupil progress and identify which steps should next be undertaken. The approach was popular because it appeared to offer a scientific basis to underpin the teaching on offer to a group of children seen as difficult to educate. However, it was also criticised as overly mechanistic and reductionist.

A second influence in the development of IEPs was the quest for an appropriate curriculum for children with SEN. As noted in Chapter 1, in Scotland children with complex needs have only been entitled to education since the mid-1970s and such children have never been easily accommodated within the mainstream curriculum. The introduction of the national curriculum in England and the 5–14 programme in Scotland intensified debate about appropriate curriculum and pedagogy for children with high support needs. IEPs fitted well with a curriculum geared toward the achievement of developmental goals. Qualitative targets geared towards the individual needs of the child could be identified and modified at the teacher's discretion. Within this formulation, the IEP was an essentially open-ended document with the emphasis on charting the pupil's progress, but with little focus on measuring or comparing attainments against standardised benchmarks.

Finally, in the US the Individual Educational Plan has fulfilled a dual role, recording learning goals for the individual child, but also recording additional state/federal resources to be provided. In the US, about 12% of the age groups have IEPs and a disproportionately high proportion of such children are black. From an equal opportunities perspective, attempts have been made to track the progress of children with IEPs and measure the relative effectiveness of different schools. It has been suggested that legal contracts should be established 'with parents as equal participants in the plan, using objective measures of goal attainments, and developing punitive consequences for failure to deliver (Goodman and Bond, 1993: 411). The legal sanctions for failure to achieve objectives was necessary because 'bureaucracies such as educational systems will move institutionally only under threat or duress' (Gallagher, 1975: 531).

To summarise, IEPs are documents which encapsulate different views of how children learn and what accountability regimes are appropriate. In terms of systematic instruction and the developmental curriculum, teaching has to be geared towards the pupil's individual learning style and goals. It is appropriate for the teacher to record teaching objectives and pupil progress, but there is no expectation that outcomes can be aggregated and used to compare the overall effectiveness of particular schools for individual or groups of children. In contrast, some commentators in the US have suggested that teaching of children with SEN in the US should be assessed using hard outcome measures and these should be used to make judgements about the effectiveness of particular schools, units and teachers. Despite these clear statements of principle, there appears to be little evidence of IEPs in the US being used for this purpose. There are a number of reasons for this, but the fundamental problem is that assessing whether a child has attained a target involves a subjective judgement. Unless great efforts are made to validate the target and the evidence for its achievement, data will always be unreliable. In addition, each child with SEN is likely to have a unique profile so that it is very difficult to compare the attainments of individuals or groups.

The purpose of IEPs

Scottish IEPs are somewhat hybrid documents. The Scottish Executive's desire to make these targets measurable and to aggregate outcomes does not appear to sit easily with their original use by special needs teachers to record individual pupils' learning goals. Different perceptions of the purpose of IEPs were very apparent among key actors whose views were tapped within different elements of the research. Scottish Executive, teachers and local authority respondents emphasised the role of IEPs in recording individual learning goals and encouraging best practice by focusing the energies of practitioners on specified objectives. Whilst teachers and local authority respondents were critical of the idea that IEP targets could be used to make comparisons of the quality of SEN provision in different settings, a Scottish Executive respondent confirmed that this was a very important part of the initiative. He pointed out that schools with pupils with SEN '. . . cannot simply be left to set their own standards and select other schools with which to compare themselves'. An inspector suggested that comparisons between special schools were important, but had to be done on a voluntary basis. Schools had been encouraged to forge links with each other and compare the nature of targets set for particular children and outcomes achieved. However, any attempt to make this mandatory would be 'howled at by the teaching profession'.

Issues in setting and reviewing SMART targets
There was consensus from a wide range of respondents that the setting of SMART targets was very difficult for many children with SEN. Among our case studies, a senior teacher of children with social, emotional and behavioural difficulties spoke of the intermittent progress made by children, which did not reflect poor teaching, but rather a chaotic home life and erratic school attendance:

> We have many cases of children who achieve to the levels that have been set and beyond and overnight they have regressed away back because of a crisis at home. That's the difficulty for many of our children, it's the baggage they bring from home, the abuse, the neglect and the inappropriate parenting that impinges on their achievement. (Senior teacher, SEBD special school)

Another headteacher commented on the difficulty of setting targets for children with degenerative conditions:

> I have no idea how somebody does that (target setting) for a child say with a degenerative disease, you know. When so much can hinge on the physical and mental well being. It must be heart-breaking and you send parents the copies of these (IEPs). How do you make targets for somebody that's so ill? (Headteacher, special unit).

There was also a perception that it was difficult to judge whether developmental and aesthetic targets had been achieved. As a result, there was a possibility that teachers would focus their attention on goals that could be measured relatively easily, and other learning objectives which were less easy to measure might be neglected. A mainstream secondary headteacher included the following comment on the questionnaire:

> It is worrying that so much administration time will be put into managing the statistics of target-setting without necessarily increasing attainment . . . It may be that raising attainment in measurable areas is at the expense of attainments in other, equally important aspects of the curriculum. (Headteacher, mainstream secondary)

Aggregating outcomes

As noted earlier, the use of IEPs was generally seen in positive terms. However, there was considerable hostility to the idea that there was any benefit at all in quantifying targets achieved and reporting school results to the Scottish Executive. A headteacher of a special school commented:

> I am absolutely convinced that we are going down the right track but I think it's fudged the benefits by throwing in all these percentages. (Headteacher, special school)

The likelihood of 'gaming' was noted, that is, the setting of targets which were easily achievable so that it could be reported that all targets had been met. A headteacher of a mainstream secondary commented:

> I think a lot of cheating will go on, I think that will basically be it. Schools will manufacture long-term targets which they know will be achievable so they look good. I think that's it in a nutshell. I don't think any school or learning centre are particularly going to go out on a wing. They're gonna play it safe. (Headteacher, mainstream secondary school)

It was evident that neither the Scottish Executive nor local authorities had any plans to moderate targets and were relying on schools to develop their internal moderating processes. Scottish Executive respondents reported that they were uncertain as to how to develop this initiative and it was possible that in the future the requirement to report outcomes would be dropped.

Involvement of key actors in the production of IEPs

The Scottish Executive hoped that, by linking the setting of targets to the production of IEPs, it would be possible to involve both parents and pupils closely in the process. Survey results suggested that in between a half and a third of schools, parents are not normally involved in the formulation and review of IEPs. Pupil involvement was particularly low in primary schools, with only 20% of schools reporting that children were routinely involved in producing and reviewing IEPs.

With regard to professional involvement, there was strong evidence that IEPs were internal school documents in which other professionals had little involvement. Class or subject teachers and learning support staff were almost always involved, whereas educational psychologists were always involved in less than a quarter of all school and special units. Health professionals were involved in the production and review of IEPs in less than 50% of schools overall and were less likely to be involved in mainstream than special schools and units. Overall, the Scottish Executive's ambition that the production and reviewing of targets would be an inclusive process involving family members and a wide range of professionals appeared not to have been achieved. The documents themselves and the learning goals remained the property of the school, with many parents expressing confusion about their purpose. For example, one parent commented:

When I was presented [with the IEP], I hadn't a clue what SMART meant and I still don't really know what it means. To me, it's just paperwork.

Target setting and inclusion
As was noted at the start of this chapter, the Scottish Executive hoped that the raising attainment and the school inclusion agendas could sit happily alongside each other and be mutually reinforcing. Three was evidence that, in some ways, IEPs with targets might magnify rather than diminish the separation of children with SEN from their peers. First, it was evident that most children with IEPs also had records of needs, so that IEPs were not being used to accommodate a wider group of children who might have some additional learning needs. A significantly higher proportion of pupils in mainstream primary (4%) than secondary (2%) had IEPs, and there was wide regional variation. Twenty per cent of pupils in special secondary schools did not have an have an IEP.

In mainstream secondary schools, it was observed by local authority and school staff that it was very difficult to involve subject staff in setting and reviewing targets and incorporating an awareness of individual pupils' targets into classroom teaching. Children with IEPs were seen as the responsibility of learning support staff. A local authority respondent expressed the fear that in the future group IEPs might be produced for secondary school pupils with learning difficulties and they might be taught a restricted curriculum in a 'remedial' class. If this were to happen, it would clearly be at odds with inclusive principles.

Finally, as noted earlier, there was considerable anxiety about the impact of reporting the performance of children with SEN alongside the performance of other children in the school. Since many parents tended to judge schools on their raw results, including children with special educational needs in the reporting of targets might have a negative impact on the public perception of the school. In the interests of inclusion, the Scottish Executive insisted that children with SEN should be included in mainstream reporting of outcomes, as well as in relation to performance on targets specified within the IEP. Clearly, for schools and the Scottish Executive, there are difficulties in reconciling the desire to value all children in terms of their individual achievements, and the recognition that socially exclusive institutions are likely to be judged as 'better' schools and selected by middle class parents.

Conclusion
Scotland has traditionally placed a great deal of importance on school self-regulation and this has been particularly marked in the sphere of special educational needs. Until recently, children with SEN could be excused form national assessments and progress was tracked on an individual basis by the child's teacher, with no external moderating or reporting. The Scottish

Executive's initiative on raising the attainment of pupils with SEN tried to introduce much higher levels of accountability into special needs education in the spirit of inclusiveness. Evidence suggests that the initiative has had mixed success. Whilst teachers approved of setting learning objectives for children with SEN as a means of improving teaching and learning, they were sceptical about whether it was feasible or desirable to aggregate such data and use it as the basis for making judgements about the effectiveness of teachers or schools. Using Power's (1997) terminology, there were fears of 'colonisation', implying that teachers might focus on those areas of the curriculum which could be readily measured and neglect 'soft' learning outcomes. Alternatively, it was suggested that in mainstream secondary schools a process of 'decoupling' might take place, so that pupils with learning difficulties might receive a restricted curriculum in a segregated setting delivered by learning support staff. It was evident that developing and reviewing targets within IEPs was seen as the preserve of school staff. Parents, pupils and other professionals were often marginalised in this process. Finally, reporting the learning attainments of children among mainstream school statistics was seen as potentially anti-inclusive, in that elite schools would find ways of discouraging children with SEN so that their position at the top of league tables would be protected. In the light of these difficulties, it appeared that there was a retreat from earlier plans to enforce strict accountability regimes in relation to pupils with SEN. At the time of writing, the Scottish Executive had not made a final decision on the reporting of aggregated targets, but it appeared likely that this requirement would be discontinued. In the future, IEPs are likely to be closely associated with Co-ordinated Support Plans, which current proposals suggest will replace records of need. This suggests a move towards the US system, where the IEP serves as an instrument to specify resources, learning objectives and as an accountability mechanism. It will be interesting to see, in the Scottish context, whether the proposed system will be able to fulfil all these functions.

CHAPTER 6

DISABILITY RIGHTS AND INCLUSION

Introduction
In this concluding chapter, we first consider the implications of the extension of the Disability Discrimination Act 1995 (DDA) to education before reviewing some of the policy tensions within the field of special needs education which have been explored in earlier chapters. Within the industrialised world, there are different approaches to protecting the rights of disabled people. The USA introduced anti-discrimination legislation for disabled people in 1990. The Americans with Disabilities Act 1990 (ADA) provided equal opportunity and access for people with disabilities, prohibiting discrimination on the basis of disability in employment, state and local government, public accommodations, commercial facilities, transportation and telecommunications. The Individuals with Disabilities Act 1990 (IDEA) related to education and, amongst other things, required schools to prepare children for adult life. Most European countries have not introduced anti-discrimination legislation, protecting the rights of disabled people by measures such as quota systems, which require organisations to include a certain percentage of disabled people within the workforce and fining them for failure to comply. Great Britain is closer to countries such as the USA and Australia, abandoning its employment quota system and introducing anti discrimination in the mid-1990s.

The Conservative government was unenthusiastic about the introduction of the legislation and blocked it many times before it finally reached the statute book. Initially the DDA applied only to the fields of employment, services and the sale or rental of property. The prohibition on employment discrimination only applied to employers with more than 15 employees in total and did not apply to members of the armed forces; prison officers; barristers; fire-fighters; employees who work wholly or mainly outside Great Britain; employees on board ships, aircraft or hovercraft; police officers. The prohibition on discrimination in the provision of goods and services did not apply to education or transport services. Furthermore, the impact of the DDA on government was restricted by s.53 DDA, which stated that anything which is done 'in pursuance of an act of parliament will be lawful even if it would otherwise amount to discrimination'.

The exclusion of education from the DDA was a source of great disappointment to the disability movement, since education is central to the future life chances of children and young people. The incoming New Labour Government in 1997 set up a Disability Rights Task Force which, in its report *From Exclusion to Inclusion* (DRTF, 1999) came up with 150 recommendations for the extension of the DDA. The Government's response to the DRTF report (DfEE, 2001) set out its plans for the extension of the DDA. These included repealing the small employer threshold, increasing the duties of providers of goods and services and extending the legislation to cover education. The Special Educational Needs and Disability Act 2001, Part 4 of the DDA, will come into effect in England, Wales and Scotland in September 2002. Two separate Codes of Practice have been published by the Disability Rights Commission to explain the legislation, one dealing with schools and one dealing with post-16 provision.

Whilst there has been some criticism of the legislation on the grounds that it uses a normative rather than a social model definition of disability and is still limited in its scope, nonetheless it is seen as very important in terms of giving political recognition to disabled people. The creation of the Disability Rights Commission in 2000 was also seen as important both practically and symbolically, signifying the Government's commitment to enforce the legislation. Gooding (2000), assessing the impact of the Act, suggests that it marks 'a huge leap forward in society's understanding of disability' and on 'disabled people's image of themselves'.

This chapter provides a brief summary of the legislation as it applies to schools and considers its future impact on justice in the field of special educational needs. Finally, it reviews some of the policy tensions which have been identified in the course of this book and considers how they may be resolved in the future.

The SEN & Disability Act 2001: Territorial coverage
Under the terms of the Scotland Act 1998, responsibility for equal opportunities is reserved to Westminster, although responsibility for the implementation of equal opportunities policies is devolved to the Scottish Parliament. Whilst Part 4 of the DDA applies throughout Great Britain (Northern Ireland has separate equality legislation), it is implemented through the separate educational frameworks of Scotland, England and Wales. Those drafting the statutory codes to accompany the legislation faced an interesting challenge in ensuring that the anti-discrimination principles of the DDA should be applied equally within the different SEN frameworks. As noted earlier, the English SEN policy framework was informed by versions of procedural justice rooted in legality and consumerism compared with the Scottish system, which was still heavily influenced by the traditional models of bureaucracy and professionalism. As the provisions of Part 4 of the DDA are put into practice, it is likely that the Scottish system will be forced to take greater account of the rights of parents and children, and it is interesting that the impetus for this shift in focus should have come from Westminster rather than Scottish legislation.

Provisions of Part 4 of the DDA

The legislation places two key duties on education providers (referred to in the Act as 'responsible bodies'). These are:

• Not to treat disabled pupils/prospective pupils less favourably; and
• To make reasonable adjustments to avoid putting disabled pupils at a substantial disadvantage.

The second duty is limited in the following ways:

• Reasonable adjustment duties do not require the responsible body to provide auxiliary aids and services;
• Reasonable adjustment duties do not require the responsible body to make alterations to the physical features of the school.

It was assumed that these areas are covered by the existing SEN framework and this point is considered further below. The type of reasonable adjustments that are required by the Act include ensuring that teaching and assessment materials are accessible to all pupils, for example, are available in large font for pupils with visual impairments or in simplified format for pupils with learning difficulties. In addition, schools will be expected to ensure that classes are in locations which are accessible. This may simply require an alteration in room allocation, so that a class attended by a disabled child takes place in an accessible ground floor location.

The duty not to treat disabled pupils less favourably for a reason relating to their disability without justification also has important implications. It means that a disabled pupil may not be discriminated against in admissions, exclusions, or in the provision of any education-related service. There are some circumstances where it may be lawful to treat a disabled pupil less favourably for a reason relating to his or her disability. For instance, if the presence of a disabled child might have a detrimental effect on the education of other children, for example, by behaving in a very disruptive or violent fashion, then the school might be justified in educating the child elsewhere. However, the local authority would need to be able to demonstrate that it had taken all reasonable steps to include the child. These might include training staff, offering appropriate support to the pupil, making adjustments to the curriculum and so on. If the local authority had not taken these steps, then it might be found to have acted unlawfully.

It is important to note that schools in the independent sector as well as the state sector are covered by the Act. Some schools in the independent sector may have traditionally paid little attention to ensuring disability equality because the existing SEN framework only applies to local authority provision. However, from September 2002 they will have to ensure, like state schools, that they do not discriminate against disabled children in any of their admissions, teaching or assessment policies and practices. Less favourable treatment of disabled children for a reason relating to their disability may be justified if it is the result of a permitted form of selection, or if there is a reason which is material to the circumstances of the particular case, and is substantial. It is clear that in the future the selection practices of independent schools are likely to be open to legal challenge.

The DDA's definition of disability
Under the DDA, a disabled person is defined as someone who has a physical or mental disability which has an effect on his or her ability to carry out normal day-to-day activities. That effect must be:

- Substantial (that is more then minor or trivial); and
- Adverse; and
- Long-term (that is, has lasted or is likely to last for at least a year or for the rest of the life of the person affected).

Physical disability is not defined, but mental disability is defined to include learning disabilities and mental health problems if these are 'clinically well recognised conditions'. This definition raises questions about whether more parents will seek to have their children diagnosed with a specific condition, such as Attention Deficit and Hyper-Active Disorder in order to gain protection under the Act. Some conditions are explicitly excluded from the Act. These include drug or alcohol addiction or dependency; hay fever; tendency to set fires; tendency to steal; tendency to physical or sexual abuse of other persons; exhibitionism; and voyeurism. Normal day to day activities include mobility; manual dexterity; physical co-ordination; continence; ability to lift, carry or otherwise move everyday objects; speech, hearing or eyesight; memory or ability to concentrate, learn or understand; and perception of the risk of physical dangers. It is worth noting that establishing disability is a major hurdle for applicants under the DDA. By way of contrast, those seeking protection under race and sex discrimination legislation do not have to undergo a similar test.

The definition of disability within the DDA is different from the definition of learning difficulties which is found in the Education (Scotland) Act 1980. Under this legislation, a child or young person is said to have a learning difficulty if he or she:

a) has a significantly greater difficulty in learning than the majority of those of his or her age; or
b) has a disability which either prevents or hinders him or her from making effective use of educational facilities of a kind generally provided in schools managed by his local authority; or
c) is under the age of 5 years and is, or would be if special provision was not made for him or her, be likely, when over that age, to have a learning difficulty as defined above.

Definitions of children in need within the Children (Scotland) Act 1995, which include disabled children and children adversely affected by disability, also differ from education and DDA definitions.

In order to know which pupils are disabled, responsible bodies and schools will have to familiarise themselves with these definitions. It is likely that some children who are covered by the DDA will not be identified as having special educational needs. For example, a child with a physical disability who can cope perfectly well with the 5–14 curriculum may not be defined as having a learning difficulty and may not have a record of needs, but nonetheless may be covered by the DDA. Similarly, a child who has been identified at schools as having a learning difficulty, for instance, a child with a mild form of dyslexia, may not be covered by the DDA.

Knowing which pupils are disabled
Under the DDA, it is up to a court to decide whether some one is disabled or not. However, responsible bodies (local authorities and schools) have to ensure that they have taken all reasonable actions to identify which children are disabled and who therefore may require reasonable adjustments. In order to be pro-active in identifying which children are disabled, schools must ensure that there is an open and welcoming atmosphere, ask parents, when they visit, whether their child has a disability and have a space on admissions forms requesting this information. If a parent has informed a school employee about a child's disability, then the school is deemed to have been informed. For example, if a school secretary has been informed that a child has diabetes, it is assumed that this information will be conveyed to all other staff in the school who need this information. If a parent or a pupil asks a school to keep confidential the fact that a pupil has a disability, or the nature of that disability, the responsible body must comply with this request. Clearly, schools and local authorities will have to review their policies on identifying disabled pupils and communicating information about them to school employees.

Relationship of the DDA to the existing SEN framework
Guidance on the new duties suggests that it is helpful to think of the legislation in terms of a jigsaw of provision, so that the new measures dovetail with existing legislation. The Education (Scotland) Act 1980 placed duties on local authorities to assess and record the needs of children with learning difficulties (see above for definition of this term). There is a duty on local authorities to provide services and resources to meet the needs of such children. The *Manual of Good Practice* (SOED, 1998a) provided advice to schools and local authorities about how to implement their legal responsibilities in a fair and efficient manner. The Standards in Scotland's Schools etc. (Scotland) Act 2000 established a presumption that all children would be educated in mainstream schools unless there were exceptional circumstances. As outlined in Chapter 1, there are imminent changes to the SEN framework signalled in the Scottish Executive's response to the consultation on assessment and recording (Scottish Executive, 2002). As noted earlier, under the DDA, the reasonable adjustments which responsible

bodies are expected to make do not include the provision of auxiliary aids and services. When the disability legislation was being drafted, it was assumed that such provision would be made under the existing SEN framework, and it was felt that making provision under two different avenues would cause confusion. However, records of needs, unlike their English counterparts, have never stipulated what additional resources will be provided. It will be important to ensure that the proposed Co-ordinated Support Plans will be sufficiently specific in relation to resource provision. If this is not the case, then the requirement of the DDA that responsible bodies make reasonable adjustments will be very difficult to enforce.

Planning duties
Since planning matters are devolved to the Scottish Parliament, the planning duties within the SEN & Disability Act 2001 do not apply to Scotland. However, as flagged up in Chapter 1, The Education (Disability Strategies and Pupils' Records) (Scotland) Bill is currently passing through the various parliamentary stages and should be on the Statute book by September 2002. This legislation places a duty on responsible bodies to publish and implement accessibility strategies for the school(s) for which they have responsibility. Accessibility is defined broadly, so that it covers the physical environment, the curriculum and communication methods. From September 2002, local authorities and schools will be expected to anticipate and plan for the needs of disabled pupils before they arrive at a school, rather than putting in place emergency measures when a pupil with a particular impairment arrives. Whilst many local authorities may have been unaware of their new duties under the DDA, they will be unable to ignore the new planning requirements and these are likely to have a positive impact on approaches to the inclusion of disabled pupils in mainstream education. It will be important that the impact of the new legislation is monitored to ensure compliance.

Redress and conciliation
Under the DDA, if a parent or child believes that discrimination has occurred, then they are encouraged to complain to the school and/or the local authority so that, if at all possible, the problem can be ironed out at an early stage. They may also contact the Disability Rights Commission for help and advice. Finally, if the matter cannot be resolved through conciliation, a case may be brought to the Sheriff Court. The Disability Rights Commission hopes to bring a number of test cases to establish legal precedents.

In England, parents have for some time had stronger rights of redress, since they have been able to being cases to the Special Educational Needs Tribunal established under the terms of the Education Act 1993. Under the Special Educational Needs and Disability Act 2001, the SENT was renamed the Special Educational Needs and Disability Tribunal (SENDIST) and its remit extended so that it would hear all cases relating to SEN and disability discrimination. The Scottish system, which involved SEN appeals being made to Scottish ministers or to Education Appeal Committees, and disability discrimination cases being referred to the Sheriff Court, appeared to be cumbersome, time-consuming and very unfriendly for users. However, the proposal for the establishment or extension of local authority mediation services and a tribunal system (Scottish Executive, 2002) appears to offer a more accessible approach to legal redress, according greater rights to children and parents. If such a tribunal system were to be established, its remit could be extended in the future to encompass disability discrimination cases.

The future significance of disability discrimination legislation
In order for the DDA to be effective in challenging discriminatory practices in education, considerable effort will have to be invested in ensuring that it is implemented according to the spirit of the law and that minimal compliance is avoided. Regular monitoring will play an important part here, but, in addition, continuing pressure on Government from disabled people and their supporters will be required. Gooding (1994) noted that 'For an anti-discrimination law to have any real capacity to achieve its goals it must be the product and instrument of a powerful collective movement' (p. 173). Anti-discrimination legislation cannot by itself dismantle structural disadvantage, but is an essential element in such change. The DDA has the capacity to widen the models of procedural justice within the Scottish SEN system, pushing the balance of power towards children and parents. There is already evidence that such moves are being challenged. For example, the members of the Association of Principal Educational Psychologists have already declared their opposition to the establishment of mediation and tribunal systems, seeing these as too adversarial. Clearly, the struggle between actors with competing agendas will continue.

Key policy tensions within the field of special needs education
We have already discussed the implications of new disability discrimination legislation in establishing new models of procedural justice within the field of SEN. These will involve new positive and negative trade-offs. For instance, socially advantaged individuals who can purchase the services of knowledgeable lawyers are likely to have more success in claiming their rights than individuals who lack such resources. Less attention may be paid to issues of collective justice when the emphasis is on individuals claiming their rights.

Categorisation versus rejection of labelling
This book has traced ongoing tensions between those who argue for the utility of categorising and identifying disabled children and those who maintain that such attempts should always be regarded with extreme suspicion. During the twentieth century, statutory categories of handicap were introduced, but were subsequently seen as stigmatising and were

replaced by the unitary category of 'special educational needs'. The DDA introduced new categories of disability based on a normative assessment of a child's mental and physical functioning rather than their educational requirements. It is inevitable that, as the new duties placed on responsible bodies are applied, tensions will arise between the different definitions of disability in education, social work and disability discrimination legislation, since each implies a different approach to assessment and identification. The definition of disability in the DDA has been challenged by social modellists, who argue that the emphasis should be on identifying the social adjustments which are required rather than individual deficits. However, operationalising a social model definition of disability within a legal structure appears to be technically challenging.

Disability: A privileged or stigmatised category?
At the root of debates over the justification for the use of categories of disability lies an uncertainty as to whether disability may be seen as a positive or negative status. The disability movement has argued strongly that it is important to see being disabled as a positive political and cultural identity, but some writers acknowledge that it is easier to feel positive about some types of impairment rather than others. For example, whilst the life of a child injured in a land mine explosion must be celebrated and enhanced, it is impossible to feel positive about the fact that this injury occurred in the first place. Such debates quickly lead into current controversies over pre-natal screening and selective abortion, where some argue that the over-riding factor has to be a woman's right to decide whether to go ahead with a pregnancy, whilst others argue that the right to life is of paramount importance and that permitting the abortion of a disabled foetus (where the normal time limits for abortion do not apply) implies that less value is placed on the life of a disabled person. Such debates are complicated by divisions within the disability movement, with some Deaf people, for example, rejecting the identity of disability and instead claiming the status of a linguistic minority.

The DDA and other social security legislation are based on the assumption that being disabled accords certain rights and privileges, such as financial support and the requirement that service providers will make reasonable adjustments to accommodate needs. However, it is unclear that the positive aspects of being identified as disabled outweigh the negative effects of stigmatisation and marginalisation. Writers like Tomlinson (1982) have warned that, whilst categorisation may appear benign, it may often have hidden malign effects and McDonnell (2000) draws on the writings of Foucault to suggest that within special educational needs attempts to categorise are likely to be accompanied by a range of disciplinary mechanisms which restrict, rather than enhance, the experience of individuals.

One way to resolve the tension between categorisation and ant-labelling approaches may be to recognise the importance of who is categorising and for what purpose. Nonetheless, systems which are initially informed by good intentions, such as the suggestion that a register should be maintained of people with learning disabilities to permit the planning of appropriate services, may subsequently be used by those with less benign intentions. It is interesting to note that, whenever efforts are made to remove categories, they appear to creep back in different forms. For example, Warnock's anti-labelling approach was followed by the emergence of 'new' disabilities such as dyspraxia, autism and ADHD.

Inclusive versus specialist provision
It is evident that the thrust of both official policy documents and legislation is currently toward including as many disabled children as possible in mainstream schools. However, some unresolved policy tensions remain in this area also. Whilst some parents feel that local authorities drag their heels in relation to inclusion, others are in dispute with local authorities because of their refusal to fund specialist educational provision for their children. Some parents of children with autistic-spectrum disorder, for instance, feel that mainstream or even generic special schools are unable to meet their child's needs, and seek placement in specialist independent schools. Parents are also keen to retain specialist qualifications for teachers of children with specific impairments, maintaining that generic qualifications or deregulation fail to provide teachers with the detailed knowledge of particular impairments and appropriate instruction techniques. New forms of segregation are also likely to emerge. For example, as noted in Chapter 4, the closure of special schools has been accompanied by the rapid increase in the number of special units attached to mainstream. A child in such a unit may have his or her name on a mainstream roll, but spend little time in inclusive settings. Whilst there is now a presumption of mainstream placement, the Scottish Executive endorses the continued existence of special schools and acknowledges the right of parents and children to request such placements. In the future, it will be important to continue to monitor the status and use of the special sector.

Raising standards versus achieving inclusion
Scottish and UK administrations are committed to the dual policies of raising standards and increasing social inclusion. It is argued that such policies should be compatible and Chapter 5 reported on an initiative geared towards including children with SEN in accountability initiatives geared towards improving learning and teaching. The research reported in Chapter 5 revealed some tensions between the policies. Setting SMART targets within IEPs was seen as a good way of sharpening teachers' approach to the education of children with SEN by focusing attention on teaching objectives and children's progress. However, attempts to aggregate outcomes with a view to assessing the relative effectiveness of different schools and sectors was rejected by local authorities and teachers on the grounds that this would

encourage the setting of easily achieved targets and the over-claiming of positive outcomes. Including children with SEN in the reporting of examination and test results was seen as promoting a tendency to exclude such children, particularly in schools wishing to maintain their position at the top of the league tables. The following unresolved paradox appears to remain in this area: if children with SEN are not included in accountability regimes, this may signal that their progress is less important than that of other children. On the other hand, their inclusion may produce unwanted exclusionary pressures within mainstream schools. This problem requires grater attention in the future.

Human capital versus social justice

Many debates in the area of special educational needs are informed by underlying, but often unspoken, concerns about how much money should be spent on the education of children with SEN compared with others. From a human capital perspective, which often dominates educational discourse, it may be argued that children with SEN may be expensive to educate but yield relatively little in terms of contributing to future national economic competitiveness. On the other hand, human capitalists have argued that some investment is necessary in the education of disabled children to ensure that they are able to make a modest living rather than being a 'burden on the state' (for a somewhat stark expression of this view, see the discussions of the Egerton Committee, reported in Chapter 1). From a social justice perspective, expenditure on education should not be calculated in relation to an individual's future profitability, but that individual's needs. Whilst special educational needs is generally described as operating a needs-led budget, Directors of Education frequently complain of budgetary over-spends in this area. Whilst it would be wrong to claim that the review of assessment and recording has been driven by financial concerns, it would be disingenuous to argue that financial concerns were irrelevant, particularly in local authority responses to the consultation. Under current legislation, incurring unreasonable public expenditure remains one of the justifiable grounds for failing to make reasonable adjustments or providing less favourable treatment to a disabled child.

Conclusion

To return to the starting point of this book, the field of special needs education provides important insights into tensions within the education system not just for disabled children, but also for their non-disabled peers. This concluding chapter has attempted to pull together the key questions which have threaded their way through the text. What version of procedural justice should pre-dominate in the management of special needs education and whose interests should be prioritised? What are the pros and cons of categorising children with special educational needs? Is a disabled identity something to be embraced or denied? Is there any place in future education systems for separate provision for some groups of disabled children? If so, what form should it take and who should it be designed for? Is it possible to devise accountability systems which include disabled children without creating perverse incentives for their exclusion? What proportion of the education budget should be spent on children with SEN relative to others? There are, of course, no easy answers to any of these questions. Solutions emerging at any particular time will involve different sets of positive and negative trade-offs. However, it is very clear that decisions about education in general, and about special needs education, will have consequences for the system as a whole. It is hoped that an understanding of this iterative relationship will inform future debates on education, and that the field of SEN is not treated as a separate cul de sac.

REFERENCES

Accounts Commission for Scotland, (2002), *Comparing the performance of Scottish Councils: Education 2000/01,* Accounts Commission for Scotland, Edinburgh

Adler, M, (1997) "Looking backwards to the future: Parental choice and education Policy" in *British Educational Research Journal*, Vol 23, No 3, pp 297–315

Adler, M, (2001) "Substantive justice and procedural fairness in social security" in *Law and Poverty* edited by Kjonstad, A, Hart Publishing, Oxford

Adler, M, and Sainsbury, R, (1991) "Administrative justice, quality of service and the operational strategy" in *Social Implications of the Operational Strategy* edited by Adler, M, and Williams, R, (New Waverley Papers — Social Policy Series No.4), Department of Social Policy, University of Edinburgh, Edinburgh

Ainscow, M, and Tweddle, D, A, (1979) *Preventing Classroom Failure: An Objectives Approach*, Wiley, London

Allan, J, Brown, S, and Munn, P, (1991) *Off the Record: Mainstream Provision for Pupils with Non-Recorded Difficulties in Mainstream Primary and Secondary Schools*, Scottish Council for Research in Education, Edinburgh

Armstrong, A, Belmont, B, and Verillon, A (2000), "'Vive la difference?' Exploring content, policy and change in special education in France: developing cross-cultural collaboration" in *Inclusive Education: Policy, Contexts and Comparative Perspectives* edited by Armstrong, F, Armstrong, D, and Barton, L, David Fulton Publishers, London

Banks, P, Baynes, A, Dyson, A, Kane, J, Millward, A, Riddell, S, Wilson, A (2001), *Raising the Attainment of Pupils with Special Educational Needs* Report to the Scottish Executive Education Department Strathclyde Centre for Disability Research, University of Glasgow, Glasgow

Barnes, C, (1991), *Disabled People in Britain and Discrimination: A Case for Anti-Discrimination Legislation* Hurst & Co, London

Booth, T (2000) "Inclusion and exclusion policy in England: Who controls the agenda?" in *Inclusive Education: Policy, Contexts and Comparative Perspectives* edited by Armstrong, F, Armstrong, D, and Barton, L, David Fulton Publishers, London

Bowers, T, and Wilkinson, D, (1998), "The SEN Code of Practice: is it user-friendly?" in *British Journal of Special Education*, Vol 25, No 3, pp 119–125

Brennan, W,K, (1974), *Shaping the Education of Slow Learners,* Routledge and Kegan Paul, London

The Cabinet Office (1999) *Modernising Government*, Cabinet Office, London

Clark, C, Dyson, A, and Millward, A, (1995) "Towards inclusive schools: Mapping the field" in *Towards Inclusive Schools?* Edited by C, Clark, A, Dyson, and A, Millward, David Fulton Publishers, London

Clarke, J, and Newman, J, (1997), *The Managerial State*, Sage, London

Corbett. J and Slee, R (2000) "An international conversation on inclusive education" in *Inclusive Education: Policy, Contexts and Comparative Perspectives* edited by Armstrong, F, Armstrong, D, and Barton, L, David Fulton Publishers, London

Corker, M, (1998), "Disability discourse in a post-modern world" in *The Disability Reader* edited by Shakespeare, T, Cassell, London

Deakin, N, (1994), *The Politics of Welfare: Continuities and Change* Harvester Wheatsheaf, London

Department for Education and Science (1978) *Special Educational Needs* (The Warnock Report) HMSO, London

Department for Education, (1994a) *Code of Practice on the Identification and Assessment of Special Educational Needs* DfE, London

Department for Education, (1994b), *Special Educational Needs: A Guide for Parents* HMSO, London

Department for Education and Employment, (1997), *Excellence for All Children: Meeting Special Educational Needs* HMSO, London

Department for Education and Employment, (1999), *From Exclusion to Inclusion; A Report of the Disability Rights Task Force*, DfEE, London

Department for Education and Employment, (2001), *Towards Inclusion-civil rights for disabled people Government response to the Disability Rights Task Force*, DfEE, London

Department for Education and Skills, (2001), *SEN Code of Practice on the Identification and Assessment of Pupils with Special Educational Needs* DfES, London

Dyer, C. (1995) The Code of Practice through LEA eyes, British Journal of Special Education 22 (2), 48–52.

Evans, J, (1998), *Getting it Right: LEAs and the Special Educational Needs Tribunal* NFER, Slough

Evans, J, (1999), "The impact of the Special Educational Needs Tribunal on local educational authorities' policy and planning for special educational needs" *Support for Learning: British Journal of Learning Support* Vol 14, No 2, pp 74–80

Fergusson, R, (2000),"Modernizing managerialism in education" in *New Managerialism, New Welfare*, edited by Clarke, J, Gewirtz, S and McLaughlin, E, Sage Publications, London

Fairley, J, and Paterson, L, (1995), "Scottish education and the new managerialism" in *Scottish Educational Review,* Vol 27, pp 13–36

Gallagher, J, (1972) "The special education contract for mildly handicapped children" *Exceptional Children*, Vol 38, pp 527–535

Garner, P, (1996), "'Go forth and co-ordinate!' What special educational needs co-ordinators think about the Code of Practice" in *School Organisation*, Vol 16 No 2), pp 179–186.

Gooding, C, (1994), *Disabling Laws, Enabling Acts* Pluto Press, London

Gooding, C, (2000), "Disability Discrimination Act: From statute to practice" in *Critical Social Policy*, Vol 20, no 4, pp 533–549

Goodman, J.F and Bond, L, (1993), "The Individualised Educational Programme: A retrospective critique" *The Journal of Special Education*, Vol 26, No 4, pp 408–422

Hargreaves, D, (1990), "Making schools more effective: The challenge to policy, practice and research" in *Scottish Educational Review* Vol 22, No 1, pp 5–14.

Harris, N, (1997), *Special Educational Needs and Access to Justice* Jordans, Bristol

Hegarty, S, (1989) "Special educational needs and national testing" in *Support for Learning*, Vol 4, No 4, pp 205–208

Heward, C, and Lloyd-Smith, M, (1990), "Assessing the impact of legislation on special education policy — an historical analysis" in *Journal of Education Policy*, Vol 5, No 1, pp 21–36

Kirp, D. (1982) Professionalisation as policy choice: British special education in comparative perspective, World Politics, XXXIV (2), 137–174.

Lipsky, M, (1980), *Street-Level Bureaucracy*, Russell Sage Foundation, New York

Male, D,B, and May, D, (1997), "Stress, burnout and workload in teachers of children with special educational needs" in *British Journal of Special Education*, Vol 24, No 3, pp 133–140

Mashaw, J, L, (1983), *Bureaucratic Justice: Managing Social Security Disability Claims:*,Yale University Press, New Haven and London

Mason, M, (1993), *Inclusion: The Way Forward; A Guide to Integration for Young Disabled Children Voluntary Organisation Liaison Council for Under Fives*, London

McDonnell, P (2000) "Inclusive education in Ireland: rhetoric and reality" in *Inclusive Education: Policy, Contexts and Comparative Perspectives* edited by Armstrong, F, Armstrong, D, and Barton, L, David Fulton Publishers, London

McPherson, A, and Raab, C, (1988) *Governing Education: A Sociology of Policy Since 1945* Edinburgh University Press, Edinburgh

Mercer, N. (2001) "Talking and working together" in *Special Educational Provision in the Context of Inclusion: Policy and Practice in Schools* edited by Wearmouth, J, David Fulton Publishers in association with the Open University, London

Merrett, F, (2001), "Helping teachers who have fallen behind" in *Special Educational Provision in the Context of Inclusion: Policy and Practice*

84	Special Educational Needs

in Schools edited by Wearmouth, J, David Fulton Publishers in association with the Open University, London

Millward, A, and Skidmore, D, (1998) "LEA responses to the management of special education in the light of the Code of Practice" in *Educational Management and Administration*, Vol 26, No 1, pp 57–66

Pickles, P (2001) "Therapeutic provision in mainstream curricula for pupils with severe motor difficulties" in *Special Educational Provision in the Context of Inclusion: Policy and Practice in Schools* edited by Wearmouth, J, David Fulton Publishers in association with the Open University, London

Pollitt, C, (1993), *Managerialism and the Public Services*, Blackwell, Oxford

Power, M, (1997) *The Audit Society* Oxford University Press, Oxford

Riddell, S. (1997) 'Education' in *Why the Poor Pay More* edited by Ffyfe, G, Scottish Consumer Council, Glasgow

Riddell, S, Adler, M, Farmakopoulou, N, and Mordaunt, E, (2000), "Special educational needs and competing policy frameworks in England and Scotland" in *Journal of Education Policy,* Vol 15, No 6, pp 621–635

Riddell, S, and Brown, S, (eds) (1991) *School Effectiveness Research: Its Messages for School Improvement* HMSO, Edinburgh

Riddell, S, Wilson, A, Adler, M, and Mordaunt, E, (2002 forthcoming), "Parents, Professionals and SEN policy frameworks in England and Scotland" *Policy and Politics*

Scottish Education Department, (1978), *The Education of Pupils with Learning Difficulties in Primary and Secondary Schools in Scotland: A Progress Report by HM Inspector of Schools* HMSO, Edinburgh

Scottish Executive, (1999), *Improving our Schools: Consultation on the Improvement in Scottish Education Bill,* Scottish Executive, Edinburgh

The Scottish Executive, (2000a), *The Same as You? A Review of Services for People with Learning Disabilities*, The Stationery Office, Edinburgh

The Scottish Executive, (2000b), *Social Justice: A Scotland Where Everyone Matters: Annual Report 2000*, The Stationery Office, Edinburgh

The Scottish Executive, (2001a), *For Scotland's Children: Better Integrated Children's Services* The Scottish Executive, Edinburgh

The Scottish Executive (2001b), *Assessing our Children's Educational Needs: The Way Forward?* Scottish Executive, Edinburgh

The Scottish Executive (2002), *Assessing our Children's Educational Needs: The Way Forward? Scottish Executive Response to the Consultation* Scottish Executive, Edinburgh

The Scottish Office, (1991 updated 1995), *The Parents' Charter in Scotland* The Scottish Office, Edinburgh

The Scottish Office, (1993), *A Parents' Guide to Special Educational Needs*, The Scottish Office, Edinburgh

The Scottish Office, (1998), *Special Educational Needs in Scotland*, The Scottish Office, Edinburgh

Scottish Office Education Department, (1987), *Curriculum and Assessment in Scotland: A Policy for the '90s*, SOED, Edinburgh

Scottish Office Education Department, (1991), *The Framework for National Testing in Session 1991–92*, SOED, Edinburgh

Scottish Office Education Department, (1992a) *Better Information for Parents in Scotland* The Scottish Office, Edinburgh

Scottish Office Education Department, (1992b) *Devolved School Management – Guidelines for Progress* Edinburgh: The Scottish Office.

Scottish Office Education Department, (1993), *Special Educational Needs within the 5–14 Curriculum: Support for Learning*, HMSO, Edinburgh

Scottish Office Education Department, (1994) *Effective Provision for Special Educational Needs: A Report by HM Inspectors of Schools* The Scottish Office, Edinburgh

Scottish Office Education and Industry Department (1996a), Children and Young Persons with Special Educational Needs: Assessment and Recording (Circular 4/96) (Edinburgh: HMSO).

Scottish Office Education and Industry Department, (1996b*) How Good is Our School? Self-Evaluation Using Performance Indicators* Edinburgh: SOEID.

Scottish Office Education and Industry Department, (1996c), *Improving Achievements in Scottish Schools: A Report to the Secretary of State for Scotland* SOEID, Edinburgh

Scottish Office Education and Industry Department, (1998a), *A Manual of Good Practice in Special Educational Needs* HMSO, Edinburgh

Scottish Office Education and Industry Department, (1998b), *Setting Targets – Raising Standards in Schools* ,The Scottish Office, Edinburgh

Scottish Office Education and Industry Department, (1999a) *Targeting Excellence : Modernising Scotland's Schools*, The Scottish Office, Edinburgh

Scottish Office Education and Industry Department, (1999b) *Raising Standards – Setting Targets. Targets for Pupils with Special Educational Needs*, The Scottish Office, Edinburgh

Scottish Parliament Education, Culture and Sports Committee, (2001), *Report on the Inquiry into Special Educational Needs* Edinburgh, Scottish Parliament

Special Educational Needs Tribunal (2000) *Special Educational Needs Tribunal: Annual Report 1999–2000*, HMSO, London

Stoll, L, (1991), "School self-evaluation: another boring exercise or an opportunity for growth?" in *School Effectiveness Research: Its Messages for School Improvement* edited by Riddell, S, and Brown, S, HMSO, Edinburgh

Tomlinson, J (1997), "Inclusive learning: The report of the committee of inquiry into the post-school education of those with learning difficulties and disabilities in England, 1996" in *European Journal of Special Need Education*, Vol 12, No 3, pp 184–96

Tomlinson, S, (1982), *A Sociology of Special Education*, Routledge and Kegan Paul, London

Vincent, C, Evans, J, Lunt, I, and Young, P, (1996) "Professionals under pressure: the administration of special education in a changing context" in *British Educational Research Journal* Vol 22, No 4, pp 475–490

Wearmouth, J, (ed) (2001) *Special Educational Provision in the Context of Inclusion: Policy and Practice in Schools* David Fulton Publishers in association with the Open University, London

Weatherley, R, and Lipsky, M, (1977), "Street-level bureaucrats and institutional innovation: Implementing special educational reform" in *Harvard Educational Review*, Vol 47, No 2, pp 171–197

Wolfendale, S, and Cook, G, (1997), *Evaluation of Special Educational Needs Parent Partnership Schemes* DfEE, London